Supply Chain Management

Amy Zuckerman

- Fast track route to understanding supply chain management

- Covers the key areas of supply chain management from inventory management and logistics to just-in-time manufacturing and just-in-time shipping

- Examples and lessons from some of the world's most successful businesses, including Compaq, Fujitsu and Staples, and ideas from the smartest thinkers, including David Bowersox, John Mentzer, David Closs and Clifford Lynch

- Includes a glossary of key concepts and a comprehensive resources guide

OPERATIONS

06.04

≫EXPRESS EXEC.COM≪
essential management thinking at your fingertips

The right of Amy Zuckerman to be identified as the author of this work has been asserted in accordance with the Copyright, Designs and Patents Act 1988

First published 2002 by
Capstone Publishing (a Wiley company)
8 Newtec Place
Magdalen Road
Oxford OX4 1RE
United Kingdom
http://www.capstoneideas.com

CIP catalogue records for this book are available from the British Library and the US Library of Congress

ISBN 1-84112-244-0

Printed and bound in Great Britain

This book is printed on acid-free paper

Substantial discounts on bulk quantities of Capstone books are available to corporations, professional associations and other organizations. Please contact Capstone for more details on +44 (0)1865 798 623 or (fax) +44 (0)1865 240 941 or (e-mail) info@wiley-capstone.co.uk

Contents

To Don and Julia

Introduction to ExpressExec

ExpressExec is 3 million words of the latest management thinking compiled into 10 modules. Each module contains 10 individual titles forming a comprehensive resource of current business practice written by leading practitioners in their field. From brand management to balanced scorecard, ExpressExec enables you to grasp the key concepts behind each subject and implement the theory immediately. Each of the 100 titles is available in print and electronic formats.

Through the ExpressExec.com Website you will discover that you can access the complete resource in a number of ways:

» printed books or e-books;
» e-content – PDF or XML (for licensed syndication) adding value to an intranet or Internet site;
» a corporate e-learning/knowledge management solution providing a cost-effective platform for developing skills and sharing knowledge within an organization;
» bespoke delivery – tailored solutions to solve your need.

Why not visit www.expressexec.com and register for free key management briefings, a monthly newsletter and interactive skills checklists. Share your ideas about ExpressExec and your thoughts about business today.

Please contact elound@wiley-capstone.co.uk for more information.

Introduction

What is supply chain management? This chapter considers the evolving nature of the supply chain. It includes:

» the driving forces of the supply chain movement;
» the role advanced technologies play in promoting this practice; and
» the move from a supply chain to a supply network.

"People now understand that you have to help business processes cross the boundaries between organizations to unleash their true value potential."

Peter Graf,[1] Vice President of Marketing at SAPMarkets

THE SUPPLY CHAIN REVOLUTION

From the United States to Asia, Europe to Africa, the demands of an increasingly competitive global economy have everyone talking about the supply chain and how to manage it better. Driven by customer demand for efficient, expedited service and the need to reduce inventory costs, the concept of managing the entire supply chain – from raw materials to delivery of finished product to the consumer – is revolutionizing the way major manufacturers, transporters and logistics companies are doing business.

Cutting-edge supply chain management not only examines ways to promote cost containment throughout the supply channel; it must also balance growing customer demand for timely and efficient service and take into account rapid changes in technology. Combined, efficient supply chain management enables a company to coordinate the manufacture and flow of products throughout the entire channel, from the supply of raw materials or components to the movement of finished goods into the customers' hands.

One approach to cost-cutting involves reducing inventories of everything from finished goods to raw materials, and reducing manufacturing cycle times through the ever-speedier delivery of goods. This effort has spawned a whole new, Web-based approach to purchasing, logistics and transportation with efforts made to ship raw materials just-in-time (JIT) for production, rather than having companies maintain large inventories of materials or components. Goods today are sought globally, not just domestically, as a means of finding the lowest-cost raw materials and components possible.

Advanced technologies – whether on the business process side or communication side – are key to today's practice of supply chain management. The use of advanced technologies helps to reduce inventories and makes just-in-time shipping possible. Employing technology wisely for well-directed information flow means that manufacturers can be nimble, producing only what stock is needed to meet service quality demand and then to continually replenish that stock. Speedy, reliable deliveries also help keep inventories at the most cost-effective level. Less inventory – or in many cases more controlled inventory – means less waste and improved profits for manufacturers. And more and more information is available on the Web, as are services that relate to supply chain maintenance, which makes for additional cost-cutting and efficiency.

Technology also affects long-range sales forecasting. The ability to access sales information on an almost real-time basis allows for quick adjustment of sales and marketing approaches. Manufacturers can look at actual sales rather than relying on forecasts made six months to a year earlier. And advanced technologies allow for the tracking and tracing of shipments on a regional and global basis. Keeping better tabs on shipments is a crucial element of just-in-time shipping.

As the use of advanced technologies becomes more widespread; as the supply chain evolves into the supply network; and as sourcing, procurement and logistics functions move onto the Web; so it becomes imperative for companies to practice efficient information management. Companies are trafficking in information, as much as in goods and services:

» information on shipment location or condition;
» information that arrives virtually in real time, allowing decisions to be made quickly to meet customer demands; and
» information that allows manufacturers to purchase raw materials when needed and produce goods as close to just-in-time as possible.

It is impossible to entirely separate logistics – what used to be called *distribution* – from supply chain management. In fact, logistics is a key piece of the supply chain. Cutting down handling time for goods as well as storage time is much of what supply chain management is all about. If the warehouse is not yet obsolete, it has more and more become a turning-around point for goods. Introducing automation into the warehouse *environment* – the industry word for the combination of computerization and bar-code-scanning technology – allows for quicker turnaround time in the warehouse and helps reduce the costs of carrying inventory.

More and more retailers, for example, electronically transmit information on inventory counts to warehouses – information that manufacturers can use to reduce production cycles. In the process, retailers and wholesalers are increasing the turn cycle, allowing them to cut costs and better meet rapidly changing customer demand. And in recent years, the growing emphasis on reducing inventories and travel time has spawned a whole new industry that is commonly called *third-party logistics*, or the outsourcing of warehousing/shipping operations to third parties. Nowadays, many third-party logistics operators – commonly called 3PLs – offer services on the Web.

COMPANIES CANNOT AFFORD TO IGNORE SUPPLY CHAIN MANAGEMENT

Companies today cannot ignore supply chain management and expect to survive. Nowadays, supply chain thinking is common operating practice for all major companies worldwide. And if just a few years ago global sourcing was available to only the largest and most successful companies, today, thanks to the Web, even the smallest companies can join online marketplaces and auctions and source goods for the best price and deal.

Dig deeper into the elements of supply chain management – from reducing inventory to implanting of advanced technologies to speed shipping, and promoting quality efforts – and you find many more companies are involved in the rudiments of supply chain management. For example, providers of electronic data interchange (EDI) technology estimate that 50% of carriers are now using such technology for messaging, tracking and tracing of goods, freight payments, and many other functions that were formerly paper-based. By the late 1990s, major intermodal providers reported that 80% of their bills of lading were received via EDI.[2]

Since the dot-com debacle of the winter of 2001, many companies – including dot-coms themselves – are returning to the rudiments of supply chain management. Those who are technologically sophisticated are implementing supply chain cost-containment basics ''through the use of inter-enterprise applications, which eliminate fat and inefficiencies from the supply chain.''[3]

Many experts believe that supply chain basics are even more important today than ever, particularly in wavering economies where even the hardiest technology firms are stumbling about seeking new direction. According to AMR Research, supply chain investments reached $5.39 billion for 2000 and will increase to $20 billion by 2004.[4]

And as technology evolves, the supply chain is evolving with it into a network of collaborative trading partners all linked electronically.

"Increasingly, manufacturers and suppliers are becoming one enterprise. The reduction in information-flow latency also permits faster product-to-market strategies. Collaborative-supply-chain communities are witnessing the breakdown of boundaries between businesses. Companies like I2 Technologies (ITWO), Manugistics (MANU), SAPMarkets, Syncra Systems, Oracle (ORCL), and others are realizing benefits as their integration applications pull all these systems together . . .

"The goal is the transformation of linear, serial supply chains into parallel, collaborative communities, dramatically reducing cycle times, improving customer relationships, and increasing productivity. In a supply chain, information is provided about inventory levels: how much inventory is available, when it's available, and so on. Benefits are obtained when companies are able to easily share forecast data, so that different companies at different points in the supply chain know how much to make, how much to ship, and when to do so."[5]

NOTES

1 Quoted in "Supply chain management: back to basics" by John Ince, *Upside Media*, June 4 2001 – reprinted in *Supply Strategy*, May/June 2001.

2 This section is adapted from *Supply Chain Survival Kit* by Amy Zuckerman, A–Z International, Amherst, MA. © 1999.

3 "Supply chain management: back to basics" by John Ince, *Upside Media*, June 4, 2001 – reprinted in *Supply Strategy*, May/June 2001.

4 Source as for note 3.

5 Source as for note 3.

What is Supply Chain Management?

Many people recognize the term "supply chain," but the precise meaning of the concept is more difficult. This chapter examines some of the classic definitions of the supply chain and its common functions. It includes:

» information on how supply chain management is both a theory and a practice;
» the driving forces that have propelled development of this field; and
» the subsidiary industries that have evolved from the supply chain.

"Overall, the trend is to get closer to the customer with a quick response system. On the other side, the aim is to reduce cycle times with the people who produce the raw materials. Then they can produce finished goods quicker to respond to the customers' immediate demands rather than forecast long-term needs. This allows suppliers and customers to produce lower inventories at a higher level of service."

Jack Kopleton, logistics consultant (former Vice President of Logistics, Philips Lighting Co.)[1]

INTRODUCTION

Supply chain management is as much a mindset as a practice. It involves looking beyond one organization and imagining all the entities involved in manufacturing and shipping a product or service, and then linking all of those entities so they can work efficiently and seamlessly as a team. That means uniting customers, suppliers, shippers, and more recently competitors, into a supply network for the most efficient use of time and resources.

There are several key functions that make up the supply chain. All functions have their own cycle times, which have to be addressed for cost containment to be achieved.

» Procurement of both raw goods and materials, as well as components, is a good place to start. Then there's the manufacturing process itself.
» The warehousing and shipping aspect of the supply chain used to be called *distribution* and is now commonly called *logistics* – often 'third-party logistics' as much of this work is now outsourced to independent contractors.
» Then there is the actual transport and delivery of goods and services, both the finished product to customers and retail outlets as well as shipment of materials required to both support a company and manufacture a product.

Once you can visualize the interaction of all these parties and functions, it is possible to move to the main purpose of supply chain management – cost containment through reduced cycle times and improved inventory management that just-in-time shipping makes possible. Yes, advanced technologies have fueled development of supply chain practices and are spurring growth of supply networks that function in a networked, Web-enabled environment. But for almost a decade many companies have practiced the rudiments of supply chain management using a phone, fax and some form of computerization and electronic communication.

As will be explored in Chapter 4, advanced technology is a crucial factor in the trend towards moving away from the supply chain and creating a supply network, which is expected to shear away additional costly inefficiencies. The availability of the Internet/Web as a transmission tool and staging platform in cyberspace for an array of supply chain functions – such as sourcing, procurement, and tracking and tracing of goods and materials – makes for additional efficiency and savings. The networked, Web-enabled world is the next stage of supply chain management – where the whole shebang is heading – but companies without these capabilities can still gain benefit from supply chain management if they focus on the following key practices:

» inventory management
» logistics
» just-in-time shipping.

INVENTORY MANAGEMENT

How best to manage that inventory for speedy shipment – weed out the bottlenecks – is one challenge that technology vendors worldwide are working on today. The old paper system that required unloading each truckload for resorting and repalleting in a warehouse is too time-consuming in today's global market.

As we will look at more closely in Chapter 4, computerized bar-coding and radio-frequency technology have evolved to the point where picking and palleting are often technology-governed. In the most advanced combination of these technologies, employees wearing minicomputers direct their warehouse picking. In the more sophisticated applications, they wear radio-frequency rings to scan bar codes for product identification rather than carry RF ''guns,'' thereby leaving both hands free for other tasks.

Software manufacturers are producing the "brains" behind the automated warehouse – the solutions that allow warehouse managers to use computers as a tool for directing the picking/palleting process. These vendors advise customers to view inventory management as a fairly consistent process that doesn't vary much from product-line to product-line. And the Internet/Web are evolving as transmission tools and cyberspace staging grounds for logistics activities, including tracking and tracing of goods and shipments. Intelligent transportation systems (ITS) are also being coupled with RF technology for speedier, more accurate picking and replenishment.

LOGISTICS

Cutting down handling time for goods as well as storage time is a key component of supply chain management. In recent years, the growing emphasis on reducing inventories and travel time has spawned a whole new industry that's commonly called logistics.

With the evolution of specialized logistics companies employing the most advanced technologies to quickly sort and ship products, there's a consequent decline in vendor- or supplier-managed inventory. Many suppliers are turning to third-party logistics companies (3PLs) to manage inventory for them, including customer migration, demands of mass merchandisers, cross-docking trends, and the growing trend of continuous store replenishment.

> "If I'm Goodyear trying to sell tires to General Motors as well as Sears, what I want to concentrate on is making the product and making a good product. I don't really want to deal with that [logistics]. Suppliers are decreasing their focus on that kind of activity and increasingly turning to third-party logistics. In the area of third-party logistics the competition is fierce because there are lots of new entrants, but the growth is phenomenal."[2]

It is hard to find a manufacturing, transport, or logistics company in the world today that is not experimenting with some form of third-party logistics. Here are some other major industry trends.

» Companies that retain in-house logistics departments are creating centralized warehouses, or hiring logistics companies to create or manage facilities for them.

» The new warehouses are automated for faster and more efficient picking and palleting. Thanks to advances in bar-coding and radio-frequency and ITS technologies, whole truckloads can be processed without any unpacking.

» Some manufacturers and suppliers with less market clout are relocating plants or distribution centers nearer to customers/suppliers in order to meet demands for shorter cycle times.

» There's growth of cross-docking operations, where material is delivered to a warehouse and then shipped out without ever going into storage.

» Computerization and information technology management is allowing companies on all sides of the supply channel to gather better information on customer demand.

» Disintermediation – or use of the Internet and other technologies – threatens to eliminate some distributors and wholesalers from the supply chain by creating direct links between manufacturers and customers.

» Technology also is making possible an inventory-reducing trend called *continuous replenishment*, which differs from industry to industry. In the automobile industry, for instance, continuous replenishment may mean that tires are shipped to meet exact manufacturing requirements.

» Cost containment is driving logistics companies to recycle – and that includes recycling everything from retail hangers to shipping containers and used laser printer cartridges. "It's become a trend because it costs more to take out the garbage than recycle it."[3]

» Whether the means of transportation is truck, air, ocean, rail, or intermodal (a combination of trucks and trains), the aim is to get shipments out on time to meet customer demands. The tools to accomplish timely, accurate shipments are various forms of advanced technologies coupled with a lot of human skill and know-how.

JUST-IN-TIME SHIPPING

"Delivering on-time performance is a major issue increasingly measured by the customer not the railway. There's a constant thrust towards cost reduction and improving customer satisfaction. That's where you start."[4]

For computer integrators like Inacom to logistics companies like Customized Transportation Inc. (CTI) and Leaseway Logistics Services, and manufacturers like Philips, the main aim today is customer satisfaction. In the realm of the supply chain, these goals translate to managing inventory and shipping to meet those just-in-time manufacturing schedules.

Take an imaginary just-in-time air shipment of computer components from Fuji, Japan, to Minneapolis, Minnesota. In the past, the manufacturer would inventory enough stock to manufacture based on six-month or annual sales forecasts. This was a hit-or-miss process, which often meant overstocking. Shipping under this sort of system was comparatively leisurely. Because of overstocking it wasn't necessary to push shippers for the fastest, most reliable delivery possible. And it wasn't necessary to keep real-time records of deliveries.

Cut back on inventories and the entire process speeds up. Purchasing must keep close tabs on inventories, be able to relay information to regional or overseas suppliers in near real time, and expect transport professionals to respond with shipments made as quickly and reliably as possible. Tracking and tracing of goods en route becomes necessary to insure that production continues without a lag.

Shippers, freight forwarders, and carriers are using a wide array of technology to speed shipments along as quickly as possibly and with the utmost accuracy. Besides satellite transmission for tracking and tracing, wireless technology for both voice and data is evolving – as is the world of intelligent transportation systems (ITS), which can be applied as a tracking and tracing tool in the warehouse and also provides passthrough clearance on highways, tolls, and even border crossings. Many more logistics and transport specialists are offering tracking and tracing services via the Web, along with other supply chain management services.

While it is still mainly the majors practicing just-in-time shipping, technology providers see the practice becoming more widespread – even for the average manufacturer and their shipper, the carrier or freight forwarder. It's not that the know-how and technology isn't there, but a matter of confidence. As they point out, no one wants to be responsible for shutting down an assembly line because of a missed order, or a missed delivery.

KEY LEARNING POINTS

» Supply chain is as much a mindset as a practice. It is a theory as well as an industry practice.
» The supply chain relates to all functions that go into manufacturing and delivery of a product, including sourcing/procurement, manufacturing, warehousing, shipping, and back-office work like invoicing.
» Cost containment is the driving force behind supply chain management.
» Just-in-time (JIT) shipping and manufacturing, which advanced technology makes possible, is the key to reducing cycle times and inventory, and can leave to massive savings.
» Logistics, or the outsourcing of warehousing coupled with shipping, is a key supply chain enabler.
» More and more supply chain functions will be handled on the Web with predictions of increased savings in the future.

NOTES

1 Quoted in *Supply Chain Survival Kit* by Amy Zuckerman, A–Z International, Amherst, MA. © 1999.
2 Mike Jenkins, then president and CEO of the International Warehouse and Logistics Association, *ibid.*
3 Diana Twede, then assistant professor in the School of Packaging at Michigan State University, *ibid.*
4 Ronan McGrath, former vice president and chief of information, Canadian National Railways, *ibid.*

Evolution of Supply Chain Management

The modern idea of the supply chain has its roots in the first production line. This chapter examines how the concept of a supply chain has evolved. It includes:

» antecedent practices that led to the full-blown supply chain theory and practice in the 1990s; and
» the evolution of a collaborative supply network.

"A few Americans made a pilgrimage to Kawasaki's Nebraska plant and created the JIT crusade (just-in-time). People didn't understand what JIT meant. They didn't realize this wasn't an inventory management system, alone."

Patricia Moody,[1] *certified management consultant (CMC), author of* Breakthrough Partnering

EARLY DAYS

It is hard to pinpoint the exact moment when the world started talking about the supply chain. But what is certain is that the term that emerged *circa* 1993 as one of the biggest, and longest-standing, industry buzzes has its antecedents in practices that date to the late 1950s and 1960s – if not to Henry Ford and the first mass-produced automobile.

The first inkling of modern supply chain practice started in the late 1950s when "people started looking at the management of goods, especially the logistics involved in inbound and outbound flows of raw materials and finished products."[2]

Most experts agree that supply chain management as it is known today emerged from the material requirements planning (MRP) efforts that major companies like Deere, Hewlett-Packard, Proctor & Gamble and others were experimenting with in the 1970s for better materials planning and control. Advances in computing power in the late 1960s had allowed companies to produce multi-level bills of material to time-phase reorder point planning on their computers. Just as important, the massive new computer programs allowed time-bucketing capability – meaning planning of material flows and manufacturing orders time buckets; this was the beginning of supply chain management analysis.

It became possible to move MRP out of the enterprise and gain more control of inbound materials from suppliers. For many companies this meant cutting back from thousands of suppliers to a choice few. It meant the beginning of outsourcing aspects of their manufacturing process, breaking down the vertical integration model that required a producer to make everything – a trend kicked off by electronics companies like Digital Equipment Co. and others.

Other experts peg the beginning of supply chain thinking to 1963 when the National Council of Physical Distribution Management

(NCPDM) was founded, which gave a staging ground for then advanced thinking on the interrelationships between warehousing and transportation functions.

> "Physical distribution management integrated these two functions, providing inventory reduction benefits from the use of faster, more frequent, and, especially, more reliable transportation. Shorter order response times via faster warehouse handling and faster transportation lessened the length of the forecast period, thereby increasing the accuracy of forecasts."[3]

The idea of coupling warehousing and transportation – what would become logistics – started to emerge during this period. Some experts consider the evolution of the logistics concept, not a major industry until the 1990s, to be a secondary phase of supply chain management. It took a number of years for procurement to catch up and become implanted in MRP, which later became a facet of supply chain management. Even into the early 1980s, many companies were still using pencils and paper for procurement.

All experts pretty much concur that major developments in managing and shipping inventory started to take off in the 1970s and early 1980s as computer systems evolved to the point where they could produce management reports and more data more frequently. Planning systems did not have to be run on batches that spewed out enormous reports full of data requiring sorting and analysis. Now transactions and purchase material records could be kept separate and integrated into the MRP system. During this period electronic data interchange (EDI) standards were developed which allowed large amounts of data to be transmitted on a closed computer network between customers, manufacturers, suppliers, shippers, and carriers. Companies started to talk about *information flow*.

At about the same time, the Japanese were championing a new manufacturing process that "pulled" material through the system and employed the basics of just-in-time manufacturing and shipping. Just-in-time requires frequent and detailed communication between customer, manufacturer, shipper, carriers, and retail outlets (if this pertains) so that inventories of raw goods, components, and finished products can be maintained at the lowest possible levels. Kawasaki's Nebraska plant became a showpiece for JIT and influenced many other American companies to imitate its processes.

THE 1990S AND THE SUPPLY CHAIN EXPLOSION

In the early 1990s, the notion of a supply chain had not entered the popular business vernacular. People talked about manufacturing or sourcing, transport trends, or distribution trends. They practiced MRP, efficient consumer response (ECR) – an early form of demand-chain orientation – and set up continuous replenishment programs.[4] But if you had mentioned the supply chain before 1993 or 1994, you would have drawn blank stares from a general business audience.

Then, almost overnight, somewhere at a time impossible to pinpoint – but *circa* 1995/96 – it seemed that the supply chain was all the craze. Trade and general business magazines devoted solely to the supply chain started to be published. Conferences with supply chain themes were all the rage. And it's been that way ever since. We have entered a phase called the "integrated supply chain."[5]

The emergence of the supply chain as a popular practice can very much be tagged to the advancement of technology and its introduction into manufacturing settings, truckers' cabs, warehouses, and retail outlets – all of which makes JIT and lean manufacturing possible. You cannot reduce cycle times effectively by manufacturing and shipping just-in-time without some form of electronic communication more advanced than the telephone. Simultaneously, there has been an increased concern about meeting customer satisfaction and quality. Supply chain management aims to deal with all of those concerns.

"It is not surprising that early implementations of demand-driven ECR focused on fast-moving consumer goods. The adoption of point-of-sale information technology, the Universal Product Code (UPC), the associated bar-coding systems and EDI standards – combined with the relatively simple manufacturing processes involved in producing most fast-moving consumer goods – make implementing demand-driven replenishment relatively easy in this sector."[6]

"It was early in the 1990s that experts started to use the term supply chain. Only the biggest companies like Motorola, Honda and other auto manufacturers were talking about a customer/supplier relationship and the supply chain. The Association for Manufacturing Excellence (AME) put together a meeting with the best people in purchasing, logistics and manufacturing – those who understood JIT and Japanese manufacturing methods and wanted to work this way with their suppliers. And the practice can thank the head of purchasing at General Motors for promoting the topic around 1994."[7]

THE EMERGENCE OF A SUPPLY NETWORK

Today it is possible to date the stages of supply chain management as pre-Web and post-Web. As noted above, by the mid-1990s the fax machine, computerization, electronic data interchange (EDI), barcoding, radio-frequency and satellite technology had evolved to a point where they could be used daily to increase efficiency and reduce wasted time and resources as part of the procurement, manufacturing, warehousing, and shipping processes. Round about 1995, it was possible to relay information, via satellite, that could be transmitted between the carrier, shipper, and customer by means of EDI. This was more cumbersome than the Web, but still a quick, efficient and viable way of relaying data and information in near real time.

The following discussions of inventory management and transport trends were written around 1998 to describe key elements of supply chain management. Note that while technology was a core element of early supply chain management, there was no mention of e-procurement or any form of Web-based services.

"The purpose of inventory management is to smooth the unknown. To take down the walls of information and see through those walls to what's happening on Macy's floor the next day. It used to be a secret and the manufacturer used to have to guess what to do. If they guessed poorly then they were out of business. We put inventory in place because of the speed bumps that naturally exist in the flow of product. Every time there's a bump meaning we oversell or undersell means a variance."[8]

"In the early days of supply-chain management there was the notion that no inventory – whether raw materials or components or finished goods – was the best and most cost-effective way to go. The trend was to reduce cycle times throughout the supply chain, push faster transportation, faster communication and faster billing. Storing product was anathema.

"But as many companies have learned over the years, the best inventory management means knowing what the best level of inventory is for your company or institution. There is some debate about what that 'right' level of inventory should be. How much inventory to maintain is a facet on how you conduct business, the computer systems in use and the planning process. Only trial and error will determine what is the 'right' amount of inventory for a given company. Experts suggest a company has to explore taking inventories down to various levels and seeing how they can function."[9]

"Experts believe that effective organization and well chosen technology can make a big difference in what inventory levels will be required to keep a business running efficiently. Technology removes human-based monitoring and inventory control and in automated warehouses allows for continual, real-time information flow between the manufacturer, suppliers, shippers and retail outlets or other customers. Daily or even hourly access to demand in stocking locations is now available thanks to computers, providing knowledge of what inventory sits in locations all the time and provide the ability to forecast over the long range. If reducing inventory to near zero levels is the ideal, better management of inventory is the reality throughout the supply chain. Within this category fall a number of different trends, from suppliers or vendors managing their own inventory to the outsourcing of logistics/distribution efforts."[10]

TRANSPORTATION BEFORE TRANSPORT DOT-COMS[11]

One of the most critical links in the supply chain is transportation. Whether shipments go by truck, rail, air, ocean, intermodal, customer demand for faster, more reliable shipping on a just-in-time or delivery-by-appointment basis is vastly altering how transport companies do business.

On both the domestic and international levels, there is an accelerating trend toward the formation of alliances to create "seamless" service whereby shipper customers can sign on with one transportation provider and receive door-to-door delivery of goods on a one-stop-shopping basis. The aim of many major carriers is to provide this service globally.

With the regionalization of distribution, suppliers are locating closer to their customers to meet their increasingly stringent time and service needs. In the less-than-truckload (LTL) sector, regional carriers and expedited carriers are finding business booming, while some of the national LTL carriers are starting to suffer. The regional transportation segment has grown dramatically because of the supply chain. Regionalization of distribution has led to shorter lengths of haul and the growth of regionalized trucking companies out to capitalize on it. This trend has some of the national LTL carriers playing catch-up to regionals and according to key industry players, will eventually lead to a shakeout in LTL carriers.

The *Journal of Commerce* points out that "North America's long-haul truckers carrying consolidated freight seem to be losing ground to their smaller, regional brethren, according to a survey of shippers." In a related trend, manufacturers and distributors have indicated they plan to ship more truck freight via United Parcel Service and Federal Express Corp., according to the study, conducted by Schroder Wertheim & Co. of New York.

The basic principles of supply chain management – customer satisfaction, cost containment, inventory management, efficient and accurate information flow, and just-in-time shipping – still pertain in the evolving networked, Web-enabled world of today. Even if all negotiating, purchasing, and business functions take place on the Web (the practice of business-to-business electronic commerce, or B2B), companies and institutions still need to produce, inventory, and ship products; not to mention manage orders, invoicing, and other financial matters.

But those on the cutting edge of this new Web world no longer talk about supply chains, but about supply networks, collaborative trading communities, and *Value Webs*. In other words, the world of the supply chain and e-commerce are merging and creating a whole slew of new business practices and a whole new way of looking at the supply chain. Consider Gartner Group's definition of c-commerce:

> "C-commerce is a form of e-business – the most advanced form. E-business has become synonymous with conducting business over the Internet. It includes a broad set of sales, marketing, and service activities that until now have been about connecting an enterprise with existing and new, immediate suppliers and customers. The c-commerce vision includes interenterprise Internet connection, but it goes a step further by enabling multiple enterprises to work interactively online to find ways to save money, make money and solve business problems – often by dynamically restructuring their relationships."[12]

There are good reasons for the grand push to B2B and a fully Web-based business, and they are very much the same motives that drove the earlier supply chain management movement:

» cost containment
» increased productivity
» customer satisfaction.

Although the online volume of buying is still low – only 0.64% of the total economy at the beginning of 2000, says the US Department of Commerce – those in the field aren't hearing many nay-sayers.

For sure, the B2B world has suffered plenty of setbacks, particularly with the stock market shakeup of the winter of 2000. Many dot-coms took a tumble and the predictions are that venture capitalists will be keeping a tight lid on startup money through the early part of the decade. Those who are financing dot-coms are demanding conventional business plans and proof of profitability, seasoned management, and other indicators that point to long-term growth.

But analysts and those operating successful dot-coms believe that B2B – not to mention an entirely networked, Web-based company – are known processes that will evolve into reality. The argument is how big and fast B2B will come and how fast total integration will come, not whether it will happen as was commonly heard in the late 1990s. Now the issues are when companies will be living B2B and how to define what "living B2B" means. Does it involve 50% of transactions? Some experts believe that world is 10 years off, some 20 and even 30 years.[13]

Whether the terms you hear are B2B, c-commerce or value-Webs, just know that the concept of the supply chain is rapidly evolving into the supply network. A supply network is the backbone of B2B. It presupposes that your own organization is fully networked so that data and information are accessible to all parties. Using the Web as a tool, you then link your networked organization to all your suppliers, trading partners, and customers for continuous data and information sharing. If peer-to-peer (P2P) technology evolves, communication may be even more direct. But even without P2P, computers from all organizations will be able to communicate directly and carry out transactions without direct human intervention.

Of course, this world doesn't really exist today. But major companies like IBM and the Big Three automakers are pushing the envelope on the procurement side, and many companies are heavily invested in software solutions that promote integration of internal functions. Others are exploring the ways to integrate all business functions with their trading partners. The US Small Business Administration reports that e-commerce is the fastest growing technological innovation. And if the small businesses are going gangbusters on e-commerce, you know that this is no mere trend.[14]

E-PROCUREMENT SHIFTING THE SUPPLY CHAIN FOCUS

In the early days of the supply chain movement, purchasing (or procurement) received scant attention. But with the shift to a B2B, Web-based world, procurement has come into its own. It is now possible to source for goods worldwide from your desktop. And it is possible to enter online auctions and exchanges without leaving your office, which means potentially massive savings for companies of all types.

With this shift of focus to B2B and procurement, there has been a shift in supply chain thinking and an elevation of purchasing from a subdivision of a company or institution to a key division which can deliver both crucial cost savings and customer satisfaction. In fact, the chief procurement officer is a new position in many companies. He or she oversees all company expenditures, and some companies have even placed their outbound logistics (warehousing and shipping) operations under the purview of this individual.

"So instead of having different functions responsible for buying incoming goods and outgoing logistics services, one function is responsible for every dollar spent. This makes the utmost sense, which is probably why it took so long to happen. In fact, most companies still have separate groups buying goods and outgoing logistics."[15]

TIME-LINE

» Today's supply chain management field evolves out of work on inbound/outbound inventory flows that started in the late 1950s.

» Material requirements planning (MRP), which entered practice in the 1970s, is considered the real beginning of supply chain practice.

» The idea of just-in-time shipping/manufacturing emerges in the 1970s/80s as computerization and electronic communication make it possible to speed up information flow between manufacturers, customers, and suppliers, allowing for speedier cycle times and reduced inventories.

» In the 1980s, Americans particularly become aware of Japanese manufacturing processes that employ JIT methods and start imitating those processes.

» Sometime around 1993/94 the actual phrase "supply chain" enters the general business vernacular.

» By 1995/96 the supply chain is all the craze. Journals and magazines are devoted to the topic. Many business graduate schools establish supply chain programs.

» The introduction of the Internet/Web in the late 1990s signals a new supply chain period – the era of the supply network. Many supply chain services, from transport to logistics, become Web-enabled.

KEY LEARNING POINTS

» Advances in technology over the last 30 years have produced the capacity to automate warehouses and create real-time information flow.
» The Japanese were the first to see the potential that technology offers, creating just-in-time (JIT) manufacturing and shipping processes, which greatly curtail the need to maintain inventory and lower costs.
» Companies worldwide moved away from vertical thinking that meant they handled all aspects of their operation – from manufacturing to shipping – to the idea of a supply chain where key functions are outsourced to third parties.
» The Internet/Web is spawning a whole new supply chain revolution, allowing real-time information flow between all members of the supply chain and creating the ability to collaborate with all parties – and competitors – in collaborative supply networks.

NOTES

1 The author acknowledges Patricia Moody as a source of some material in this section, as well as Dr John Mentzer and Peter Metz (see notes 2 and 3 below).
2 The source is an interview in June 2001 with Dr John T. Mentzer, Bruce Chair of Excellence in Business, Department of Marketing, Logistics and Transportation, University of Tennessee.
3 From "Demystifying the supply chain" by Peter Metz, *Supply Chain Management Review*, winter 1998.
4 See "After supply chains, think demand pipelines" by Fred Hewitt, *Supply Chain Management Review*, June 11 2001.

5 Source as for note 3.

6 Source as for note 4.

7 Patricia Moody, *ibid.*

8 Richard Weitz, then director of continuous replenishment, Johnson & Johnson, quoted in *Supply Chain Survival Kit* by Amy Zuckerman, A–Z International, Amherst, MA. © 1999.

9 Jeff Schutt, partner in CFC Consulting, *ibid.*

10 From the author's *Supply Chain Survival Kit*, A–Z International Associates, Amherst, MA. Copyright © 1999.

11 *Ibid.*

12 From the author's *Tech Trending* in the ExpressExec series.

13 Kevin Fitzgerald, editor-in-chief of *Supply Strategy* magazine, *ibid.*

14 See note 12.

15 See note 13.

The E-Dimension of Supply Chain Management

Moving from a supply chain to a supply network presents new challenges for companies. This chapter explores the key issues, among them:

» how the Web is affecting procurement and what makes sense for your company;
» how many transport/logistics services are now available online; and
» whether e-sourcing is the best route for your organization.

"Supporting the complete sourcing cycle will require companies to configure the appropriate mix of technologies, strategy and product and supplier expertise into an e-sourcing framework that addresses four key processes."

Tim Minahan,[1] *Director of Supply-Chain Research, Aberdeen Group, Boston, MA*

INTRODUCTION

What happens when you take basic supply chain principles and apply them to a networked, Web-enabled organization that works with suppliers and customers with similar technology capabilities? You have the beginning of a supply network.

Although many companies are experimenting with Web-based services and facets of electronic commerce – particularly e-transport, e-logistics, e-sourcing, and e-procurement through Web-based marketplaces and exchanges – only a small percentage of companies worldwide actually have the capabilities to operate in a supply network environment. Many depend on a variety of technologies strung together with technological band aides called "middleware". Some may not have moved much beyond basic computing and a dedicated e-mail line.

Transferring supply chain activities to a Web environment is very much in its infancy. Even so, the big research and analysis firms predict huge cost savings as manufacturers, their supply base, customers, and shippers/logistics operations evolve supply network capabilities. This chapter looks at how e-transport, e-logistics, e-sourcing, and e-procurement are progressing.

E-TRANSPORT

Because transportation and logistics are so crucial to maintaining material goods and product flow in this new economy, these industries are using technology in enormously creative ways. Basic computing, satellite technology, radio-frequency, bar-coding, cellular, X-rays, intelligent transportation systems (ITS), and now the Internet – just about every technology imaginable – is being combined to literally and figuratively drive the supply network. It would not be possible to source goods, track shipments, inventory goods, or send freight bills on a real-time basis – let alone on a global basis – without advanced technology.

Moreover, the Internet and Web are having an enormous impact on the transportation industry. For example, the rush to cyberspace shopping has created a bonanza for expedited overnight carriers like FedEx and UPS. These same carriers have been at the forefront of moving many of their business functions to the Web. And there has been a huge push to develop Web-based transportation dot-coms where all business transactions take place on the Web. However, only a handful of the pioneering transportation and logistics dot-coms are expected to survive into maturity.

Transportation visionaries see the Web being used more and more to manage real-time operations. For truck fleets, the sort of optimization software that is already allowing the big companies to better manage truck capacity, ensuring that all space is utilized each delivery, will be available via the Web to smaller companies.[2]

For example, transportation and logistics leaders are joining forces to launch operations like SupplyLinks, which involves seven leading global transportation and logistics providers joining forces to offer procurement and transportation management services on the Web. Other SupplyLinks services include exception management across modes, carriers, and service levels to quickly identify delayed shipments and other in-transit issues.

Another company plying its services on the Web is Mobility Technologies, a provider of digital traffic and logistics information. One product allows motorists in heavily congested areas to better plan routes and avoid congestion, which aids in just-in-time deliveries.

As the Internet merges more with intelligent transportation system (ITS) technologies, this sort of scenario could be common: With one transponder connecting to a roadside reader and a networked system in the cab, the truck drivers of the future will be able to pass through any toll booth in the country, plus gain pre-clearance for safety checks en route, access online navigation advice, and even order food without having to pay cash. All that will happen with the combination intelligent transportation systems, in-vehicle networking, and computing.[3]

E-LOGISTICS

The US industry, alone, spent an estimated $950 billion on logistics activities in 2000 and the industry reportedly wants to cut costs in this area. But experts point out that the third-party logistics industry is lagging when it comes to e-technology and "must now speed up efforts to acquire technology that will enable it to electronically aggregate shipments, help customers visualize inventory levels, deploy transportation assets or save costs by consolidating shipments."[4]

There are exceptions, of course. AMR Research cites third-party logistics (3PLs) giants – like APL Logistics, BAX Global, C.II. Robinson Worldwide, Exel, and TNT Logistics North America – as examples of "e-enabled" companies. Companies like Descartes Systems and Freight quote.com are providing online logistics services. FrieghtMatrix offers an ASP (application service provider) model that provides virtual 3PL and supply chain services. And companies like DSC Logistics and Ingram Micro Logistic are now offering e-fulfillment.[5]

Progress is also being made in the software arena to develop Internet-based models for the industry, particularly for small-to-medium shippers, while larger 3PLs are focusing on developing programs for Fortune 500 companies. Many 3PLs, however, have been slow to adopt existing technology because of lack of investment funds and the difficulty of attracting top IT professionals to run their services. And many carriers and other 3PL customers just aren't technology-enabled enough to take advantage of Web-based services.

THE STATE OF E-LOGISTICS[6]
» The e-logistics landscape is still highly fragmented.
» The role of third-party logistics providers (3PLs) is changing from tactical to strategic.
» Logistics exchanges are moving from the fringes to the center of logistics management.

E-SOURCING

Sourcing for goods and services is a crucial part of the supply chain, yet one that until late has resisted automation. For many companies, finding the best materials or services at the best price and under the most advantageous shipping arrangements is a laborious process. There are many instances where human knowledge and interaction make a difference. The fact that many companies resist using advanced technology or automating their sourcing activities has made e-sourcing slow to catch on.

And yet, the Aberdeen Group in Boston has identified sourcing as the most effective lever for designing highly efficient supply chains.

> "It is during the sourcing process that the cost of an organization's products and the structure of its supply-chain network are defined. Effective sourcing reduces costs, improves quality and speeds time-to-market cycles … Internet-based sourcing automation, or e-sourcing, can streamline strategic sourcing by creating highly efficient and collaborative online negotiation environments that deliver."[7]

E-sourcing includes using Web-based technologies to automate and streamline the identification, evaluation, negotiation, and configuration of the optimal mix of suppliers, products, and services into a supply chain network that can rapidly respond to changing market demands, reports the Aberdeen Group. This emerging market includes "pure-play" e-sourcing solutions, reverse auction or dynamic trading technologies, supplier intelligence services, and tools as well as procurement service providers.

> "Supporting the complete sourcing cycle will require companies to configure the appropriate mix of technologies, strategy and product and supplier expertise into an e-sourcing framework that addresses four key processes."[8]

E-PROCUREMENT

Experts believe that the potential savings that e-procurement offers manufacturers is "staggering." Some of the most significant benefits include:[9]

» reduced transaction costs, in an area of the total spend that dwarfs what's spent on indirect goods;
» reduction of stocks of obsolete products and inventory for those products, owing to more timely reaction of supply to demand;
» reduced inventory levels in general, through reduced cycle times;
» quicker reaction to changing market trends, enabling a manufacturer to gain a competitive edge in new product development; and
» redeployment of procurement and other professionals away from transaction processing activities toward work that is more strategically important to market success – such as global market research and analysis, long-term negotiations with strategic suppliers, supplier development, and researching of new-technology tools that can elevate procurement and supply chain management performance.

It is important to note that some types of direct materials are more suited to e-procurement than others. And dispel the notion that most e-procurement systems installed to date have been designed solely for indirect goods and materials-office products, as well as MRO (maintenance, repair and operation) supplies. The high-tech manufacturers, for example, have been using the Internet to purchase materials used in their manufacturing processes – direct materials – for a number of years. There are booming exchanges in the aerospace industry, like Exostar, that offer online purchasing capabilities to that industry. The same goes for automotive goods where it is possible to purchase goods related directly to production.

Even so:

> "... most manufacturing industries have not shifted their direct materials procurement to the Internet. There are many reasons for the slowness in adoption, not the least of which are the fear of using new systems in this critical area and the reluctance of suppliers to become e-commerce capable. But simply put, the Internet has the potential to fully integrate manufacturing supply chains, from the point raw materials come out of the ground to final disposition of the product."[10]

A recent e-procurement study – by the Center for Research in Electronic Commerce at the University of Texas – of 1200 American and European companies indicates that a number of large companies are already reaping tremendous benefit from e-procurement. The study, funded by computer manufacturer Dell, looks at how manufacturing, retail, and wholesale companies are conducting e-procurement. It addresses the effect that e-business "drivers" – like system integration, supplier-related processes, and supplier e-business readiness – had on financial measures such as revenue per employee, gross margin, return on assets, and return on investment.

Not surprisingly, companies that openly share information, plans, and demand forecasts with their suppliers have been found to be the best positioned to take advantage of Web-based buying. Some companies identified as promoting supplier communication include General Electric, Cisco Systems, Home Depot, Dell, and The Boeing Co. On the other hand, companies that do not take quality supply continuity very seriously, and don't work on supplier communication, are not prepared to take advantage of Web buying. These same sort of companies are not investing in IT functions such as automatic invoice processing and online status verification of procurement orders, which means they are being left out of the Web loop.

"If they don't do the right things, technology by itself doesn't help much. You might have wonderful technology, but has anything else changed? No. That is why some companies are in deep trouble."[11]

SOME E-PROCUREMENT TIPS

Before spending one penny on technology, executives wishing to implement e-procurement and supply chain management systems should:

» consult with key suppliers;
» examine and possibly change inefficient business processes; and
» invest in "e-business drivers" that maximize financial returns.

Supply executives must convince suppliers that they will change their own company's inefficient practices, and they should do this before they make major technology investments. If they don't, they're probably wasting their money.

BEST PRACTICE CASES

From the Big Three automakers to companies like Diversified Systems in Indianapolis, companies are sorting out best practices for moving into a Web-based supply network. Here are some examples from these companies and others.

Improving order response, tracking capabilities, shipping accuracy, and timing from suppliers

Subaru–Isuzu's US operation is working on improving order response and tracking capabilities for after-market products, and improving logistics visibility for non-EDI production parts suppliers is the focus of Subaru–Isuzu's pilot e-procurement program.[12] Improved shipping accuracy and timing from suppliers is also key. The focus is the auto company's service parts and production parts logistics business. All suppliers will provide electronic advance shipping notices to Subaru–Isuzu. Planners will track shipments to Subaru of America distribution centers. They're using a solution called VendorSite from Eventra, and developing a Microsoft platform for it.

Focus on e-training

Like other companies implementing e-procurement systems, Subaru–Isuzu has found that not all suppliers are ready for e-commerce, and that a good deal of training is needed. Both Subaru–Isuzu and their vendor, Eventra, conduct on-site training sessions if necessary.

Providing backup support when rolling out solutions

Eventra is setting up a "24/7" e-mail and phone system to provide support to suppliers. The company's information systems group will have a designated support contact to help suppliers, and will put in place feedback mechanisms to help suppliers with implementation.

Putting materials management on the Web

Electronics contract manufacturer Diversified Systems specializes in fabrication and assembly of printed circuit boards and is an early adopter of Internet-based e-procurement.[13] Using a combination of inhouse and outside efforts – from Digital Market, later acquired by Agile Software – the company now handles its materials management on the Internet, using Ariba Buyer to interface with its distributor suppliers.

The system automatically checks for validity of parts numbers before a quote goes out to distributors. When each distributor receives the quote, built-in safeguards have already ensured that they see only their own part numbers, and that each one is in stock. Diversified Systems now produces well over 100 quotations per month, which has greatly increased productivity. It used to take three or four days to produce one quotation.

Organization is key in the switchover to the Web

Use a small, multidisciplined team with a senior management member leading the team when automating processes, or moving them onto the Web. The team should consist of members from MIS (management information systems), procurement and technology, at the least.

Data management is increasingly important

Intelligently storing and managing all the data your new business-critical applications can generate will separate those who thrive in the information age from those left in the dust. Whether it's enterprise resource planning, electronic business, or business intelligence, you have to turn information into a strategic corporate asset. Its value to the organization and the bottom line is often directly related to how easily this information can be shared across the entire enterprise and beyond – including customers, suppliers, and other trusted business partners. Companies like TQnet Inc. in Orlando, Florida, are starting to provide online services that allow other companies to access data management solutions from the Web.[14]

Web conferencing

Companies as diverse as the Big Three automakers, Nortel Networks, and Texas Instruments have all learned the hard way that technology is no substitute for face-to-face communication when trying to maintain global supply chains. If travel is impossible, these companies and others are exploring a wide variety of Web conferencing tools that allow for real-time communication from your desktop. Some solutions even allow for a party in Hong Kong to make a presentation to participants worldwide.

EVOLVING THE SUPPLY CHAIN INTO A SUPPLY NETWORK

The following are a few examples of how supply chain concepts have evolved.

Internal organizational communication

» *Supply chain technology* – Telephones and faxes.
» *Supply network technology* – E-mail and company/institution intranets, and Web-enabled cell phones allow you to share information and communicate while on the go.

Business process communication

» *Supply chain technology* – Business data and information flow from department to department via e-mail and enterprise resource planning (ERP) software.
» *Supply network technology* – New standards for business-to-business communication will allow the transmission of everything from invoices to reports throughout a supply network. Peer-to-peer (P2P) software will allow you to network with millions of computers worldwide without the need for a browser.

External communication

» *Supply chain technology* – Telephones, faxes and electronic data interchange (EDI), aided by the Internet as a transmission tool.
» *Supply network technology* – New standards will eventually eliminate EDI messaging sets and allow company and institutional computers to communicate directly.

Computing

» *Supply chain technology* – Mainframe computers dominate to store massive amounts of data.
» *Supply network technology* – Networked systems that rely on servers are supplanting mainframe computers. Servers are being connected to Web browsers to allow data and information to flow directly to cyberspace. Peer-to-peer software may make the browser unnecessary, if not obsolete.

Purchasing

» *Supply chain technology* – Telephone, faxes, and EDI.
» *Supply network technology* – The Web is becoming the place where purchasing managers can source goods electronically. As Web languages evolve, computers will handle purchasing directly.

Inventory management

» *Supply chain technology* – Computerization aided by EDI, and now the Internet, has allowed information to flow from warehouses to manufacturers and shippers so that all parties have accurate, real-time inventory counts and can manufacture and ship just-in-time.
» *Supply network technology* – Advancements in radio-frequency and bar-code technologies, and the introduction of remote messaging technologies, allow for instantaneous stock counts with the wave of an RF wand.

Shipping

» *Supply chain technology* – Telephones, faxes, and EDI are coupled with computing, as well as satellite, global-positioning and cellular technologies, to allow for near real-time global tracking and tracing of goods.

» *Supply network technology* – The introduction of the Internet as a data transmission tool means that real-time information is now available. Intelligent transportation systems (ITS) coupled with computers are moving goods more quickly along highways, promoting safer transportation and providing passthrough capabilities at border crossings. And transportation and logistics services – including real-time tracking information and software products – are now available on the Web.

KEY LEARNING POINTS

» The big push in supply chain thinking is the move from a supply chain to a supply network mentality.

» Companies may lack the advanced technology to operate in a supply network environment, but can start thinking and planning for a collaborative trading future.

» Four key supply chain functions – transport, logistics, sourcing, and procurement – can now be conducted on the Web.

» Moving goods just-in-time means concentrating on improved order response, tracking capabilities, shipping accuracy, and timing from suppliers.

» Training becomes crucial. Employees need to learn how to function in a collaborative e-environment.

» Backup support matters when rolling out new solutions to push that supply chain into a supply network.

» Organization matters even more when you move services into cyberspace, and data management is something all companies need to practice.

NOTES

1 ''Strategic e-sourcing: negotiating a winning supply chain – views and analysis from leading supply management consultants and analysts'' by Tim Minahan, *Supply Strategy*, online edn, May 2001.

2 For more detail, see p. 116 in the author's book *Tech Trending*, in the ExpressExec series.

3 *Ibid*, p. 117.
4 See "Logistics service providers fall short in Web enablement," *Supply Strategy*, May 2001. The sources are John Fontanella and Chris Newton, of AMR Research, Boston, MA.
5 *Ibid*.
6 *Ibid.*
7 See note 1.
8 See note 1.
9 The source is "Online procurement of production materials can streamline procurement processes and integrate supply chains" by Kevin R. Fitzgerald, *Supply Strategy*, May 2001.
10 See note 9.
11 "E-procurement: what to do first," *Supply Strategy*, online edn, June 2001. The source is Prabhudev Konana, assistant professor at the Center for Research in Electronic Commerce, University of Texas. The boxed tips that follow are from the same source.
12 See "Putting the direct buy online" by Kevin Fitzgerald, *Supply Strategy*, June 2001. The sources are William Howard and Tim DeLong of Subaru–Isuzu.
13 See "Putting the direct buy online" by Kevin Fitzgerald, *Supply Strategy*, June 2001. The source is Stan Bentley of Diversified Systems.
14 The source is Jim and Rick Harrington, on the management board of TQnet Inc.

The Global Dimension of Supply Chain Management

Even those companies that don't import or export are affected by global practices. This chapter explores how to operate a global supply chain and what matters to organizations of all types. Issues include:

» a look at how foreign cultures and languages matter;
» the role that import/export compliance and standards/testing practices play as hidden supply chain forces; and
» knowing how to stay in touch in real time on a global basis.

There is a case study of Sandvik Coromant Co.

"No one transportation provider can offer the best service to every destination in the world. You're going to have to put together a menu of services that will best fill your needs."

Jack Hanlon,[1] Vice President of Logistics, Sandvik Coromant Co.

INTRODUCTION

With international markets opening, more and more companies are finding they have to think global to maintain a competitive edge. Some experts contend that companies must think global, even if their products never leave native shores.

"You can't get through a day without the global economy touching you. It's something companies have to be aware of and planning for. Global supply-chain management is key to sustainable competitiveness in a global economy. It's one of the few areas where you can do two things – reduce costs and improve customer service."[2]

When companies move into the global arena, their supply-chain problems multiply exponentially. Consider the case of Sandvik Coromant Co. – a Swedish manufacturer of cutting tools with extensive North American and Latin American presence – that works hard to move its product from central locations to many different countries around the world on a just-in-time (JIT) basis. Because their product is key to the manufacturing process of large industrial operations where downtime is prohibitively costly, there's little leeway in Sandvik's global shipping schedule.

To manage a supply chain across an ocean and between two continents means being highly organized. There is no room for error at border crossings. Establishing reliable worldwide transportation is a must. Both areas have proved difficult for the Swedish company.[3]

As the Sandvik example indicates, many new issues arise when a company takes a supply chain global. Besides the obvious transportation and logistical concerns, there are hidden forces that can swamp a global supply chain. Cultural and language barriers must be overcome. Import and export requirements must be met, along with foreign regulations.

International standards and testing practices can surface that will also hamper the free flow of goods. Move the supply chain onto the Web and then issues of privacy and fraud arise, as well.

And then there are a slew of management issues to address, some of which relate to the use of high technology and others which are strictly human. Remote management provides challenges that advanced technology can help alleviate, but not without some human intervention. And there are myriad products flooding the market that promote electronic global communication.

These are all the hidden forces of the supply chain that are often overlooked as the experts discuss cycle times and push and pull supply chain flow. All the theory in the world will not get your supply chain off the ground if your goods are stuck in customs warehouses around the globe for lack of compliance to relevant regulations, standards, and testing practices. This chapter looks at some of the issues that come to play when operating a global supply chain.

CULTURAL AND LANGUAGE BARRIERS

Companies that have underestimated the power and force of cultural differences and language barriers have paid in the global marketplace. Major corporations from Xerox to Texas Instruments have long learned that they must address language barriers, not to mention more global communication concerns, if they are to keep supply chain information flowing properly.

Cultural differences can be extremely subtle. When working with an import/export concern with clients in the Netherlands, this author learned first-hand that there can be different values and work practices functioning even in western countries that appear to be so similar to the United States. In one case, class stratification came into play and an employee balked at approaching a client he considered to be "aristocratic."

In parts of the Middle East, Latin America, and Asia it won't be uncommon for business people to encounter what is commonly known as "payola." Some seasoned business people have been known to build in the customary bribes to government officials and others when dealing in countries like China, even though this is strictly illegal under US law.

IMPORT/EXPORT COMPLIANCE

Companies do not have to be directly involved in international trade to find themselves meeting import/export requirements. If they supply manufacturers that sell overseas, they may very well find they have to comply with US or foreign regulations. Moreover, the chain of responsibility for non-compliance extends farther along the supply chain than in the past, which means that all parties to an overseas transaction – suppliers, manufacturers, and shipping professionals – must ensure that regulations are met.

Export regulation experts warn companies that want to manufacture and ship just-in-time that they best have their import/export compliance in top order if they want to meet those sorts of deadlines. Once in the field, things can get "pretty crazy" for a buyer's supply chain when specs are off, or when the documents accompanying a shipment are not in order for the goods to clear either US or foreign customs.

"How in the world can you begin to develop a supply relationship with an overseas client if your goods are rejected before they even enter the country? That means you're compromising the foreign client's flow of goods and no client is going to stand for that. When your supply chain is interrupted, your competition is always there to take away your customers. It takes years to build up the reputation of your business."[4]

The burden falls on importers and exporters to constantly track ongoing regulation changes both in the US and in foreign markets. They must also keep up with domestic and foreign regulations that affect packaging, labeling, public health, and the environment. Once again, there is no point in operating a seamless manufacturing and distribution system, only to have goods held up at border crossings.

STANDARDS AND TESTING PRACTICES

Standards are the underpinning of manufacturing design. Testing practices provide customer assurance that a product has met health, safety, and environmental standards and/or government regulations. These practices are the glue that is binding a new global economy, but when misused they can be potent economic weapons that the World Trade Organization (WTO) has identified as an emerging non-tariff trade barrier.

When companies fail to comply with national or regional standards and testing requirements, they can find themselves shut out of markets. Once again, the supply chain breaks down. This has been the case in Europe where the European Union's CE Mark for health, safety, and the environment is now a requirement for market entry. China has its own version of the CE Mark and its agents have been known to deny market entry for products that lack this seal of approval.

WTO officials are also tagging the ISO 9000 international quality assurance standard and ISO 14000 environmental management system standards for evidence that they are proving to be non-tariff trade barriers in countries that have referenced these usually voluntary standards into government regulations. This is the case in the EU, for example, where ISO 9000 is the required quality base for industries such as pacemakers and computer switches.

A related consideration are the international standards and testing practices, which the WTO has identified as an emerging non-tariff trade barrier. Companies that do not comply with foreign standards and testing protocols may find their product entry delayed. Even worse, they may find themselves entirely shut out of foreign markets. And once again, the supply chain breaks down.

The issue is deceptively far-reaching. In fact, manufacturers don't have to leave home, or even be involved with foreign manufacturers, to face international standards requirements. For example, many American multinationals have made the ISO 9000 international quality assurance standard a requirement for their domestic suppliers. In some cases, the European CE Mark for environmental health and safety may be required for component parts, and that's whether a company trades directly with Europe or supplies a company doing so. The CE Mark is a label in the US that companies affix to products as a statement of conformity to European requirements.

Organizations such as the American National Standards Institute (ANSI) and standards bodies worldwide can provide information on what standards and testing practices matter to your company in overseas markets.

ADVANCED TECHNOLOGY

Although human interaction is crucial to maintaining solid global communications and human skills imperative to managing information flow of the supply chain, no company will be able to practice global supply chain management without advanced technology – see Chapter 4 on the e-dimension.

There are a whole array of options companies can choose from to better manage their individual financial flow – what is commonly called "enterprise resource planning" or ERP. Software solutions also abound for just about every supply chain function, from planning to warehouse inventory management and shipping. The next generation of ERP products is aimed beyond the single enterprise and manufacturing sector to encompass the entire supply chain and also service companies. And many of these solutions are starting to be offered on the Web through ASPs (application service providers).

Until recently, the most common message set for supply chain information has been electronic data interchange (EDI). EDI allows for transmission of vast quantities of data at high speeds in a secure fashion. With the advent of the Internet and Web, many companies are utilizing the Internet as a transmission tool and for retaining EDI message sets. In time, this combination of EDI/Internet could be replaced by a new generation of Web-enabled ERP software systems and applications that handle all supply chain functions, and provide electronic commerce capabilities. This switchover will promote what experts call "intelligent networking," which will allow flexible intercommunication between global networks.[5]

Add in new wireless capabilities, including the advent of Web-enabled phones, and it won't be too many years before more and more supply chain information applications will be managed remotely. There are already many examples of functions such as printer operator panels where configuration isn't performed manually.

Sandvik Coromant Co., for example, is already practicing a form of electronic remote logistics management utilizing three PCs with lots of computing power. This equipment stores and transmits data for the company's three distribution centers – two in Europe and one serving North America. Inventory tracking is managed from these centers, which then serve the global operation.

INFORMATION MANAGEMENT

No one manages a global supply chain without being concerned for how information flows through whatever advanced technology tools a company puts in place. Accuracy is particularly crucial to just-in-time shipping and inventory control. Inaccurate information, missing data, and late shipments can throw off an entire supply chain.

In surveys this author has conducted in recent years, producers of shipping and logistics-related software find that customers most commonly fail to send out complete information, or to produce much-needed data in a timely fashion. Shipping notices often arrive with 20% of the data missing, and 20% of the time a customer will not indicate when a shipment has left port – or a report is made many hours later.

Although advanced technology can provide some built-in accuracy checks, employees need to be trained to better manage information. Managers from companies like Texas Instruments, Bell Helicopter, and Coopers & Lybrand all believe that providing some basic reading, writing, and analysis skills can also improve supply chain information flow. They know that managing a supply chain, particularly on a global basis, is about:

"... teaching people to zero in on critical insights and how to leverage and apply those insights. There seems to be a belief among information technology (IT) professionals that if they can just get a better search engine ... then those systems will be able to do what a great analyst can do, but what separates great analysts from OK analysts is that great ones have the ability to see what others don't. There's an ability to see patterns and to see what lies outside the patterns."[6]

BEST PRACTICE CASE

Dole Food Company[7]

Working out of smaller ports, rather than larger facilities, has always paid off for Dole Food Co. But in 2001 the food giant stunned everyone in the industry with the announcement that it was re-evaluating its logistics strategy and moving from the port of Los Angeles to the port of San Diego, both in California.

The world's largest producer and marketer of fresh fruit and vegetables recognizes that the port of Los Angeles is a major gateway and distribution point for the western US. However, company officials understand that both Los Angeles and the nearby port of Long Beach were experiencing growing pains as imports – especially from Asia – continue to reach record highs.

As an entirely vertical company that controls everything from the growing of the products to delivery to final destinations, Dole Food Co. is very dependent on the transport part of its business to maintain a competitive stance. Over the years, the company has found that utilizing small ports makes for more efficient management of its supply chain.

Working with smaller US ports is part of the company's strategy, as is maintaining good relationships with all ports the company utilizes. Company officials say the port of San Diego – roughly 100 miles south of Los Angeles – presented the right opportunities at the right time. Port authorities are promising the company top-notch service and attention, plus they boast the largest on-dock cold storage facility on the West Coast of the US.

Dole Food Co., in turn, is investing $25 million to develop a prime port facility in San Diego to be complete in the fall of 2002. Under the plan, the port of San Diego will develop about 20 acres of its Tenth Avenue Marine Terminal for the company's operations. Besides a 9400-square-foot office building and maintenance shop, there will be a container and trailer wash facility and gatehouse.

Company officials reportedly are pleased with the attention and say that San Diego makes them feel like "a big fish in a small pond rather than a small fish in a big pond."

Dole Food Co. is hardly San Diego's only big tenant – or tenant-to-be. The National City Marine Terminal has an advanced vehicle import/export facility and handles Acura, American Honda, Isuzu, and Volkswagen.

KEY LEARNING POINTS

» Companies need to think global to survive. Even if your goods never leave your national boundaries you will be affected by the regulations and testing practices of other countries and regions.

» Maintaining a global supply chain means focusing on communication (including foreign languages), foreign cultures, transportation, and national/regional regulations and testing/standards practices.

» You can underestimate the importance of learning the cultures of the markets where you are doing business overseas. Having employees who are fluent in the language of that region is one key to success.

» Import/export regulations exist worldwide. Someone in your company must have an expertise in this field or your global supply chain will break down at the border.

» Many countries have their own environmental and packaging regulations. Your supply chain will falter if you don't meet those requirements.

» Standards and testing practices can function as hidden regulations. This is an area where expertise counts to keep goods flowing in a global supply chain.

» Advanced technologies will be key to maintaining as close to real-time communication as possible around the globe.

» No one manages a global supply chain without keeping information flowing quickly and accurately throughout your global network.

» Don't forget the need to travel and have face-to-face meetings with foreign managers, employees, and alliance partners.

NOTES

1 Quoted in "It's not a small world after all" by Amy Zuckerman, *Supply Chain Technology News*, Sept./Oct. 1999, pp. 30–32.

2 Jean Murphy, editor of *Global Sites and Logistics* magazine, quoted in the author's *Supply Chain Survival Kit*, A–Z International, Amherst, MA. © 1999.

3 See note 1.

4 Fritz-Earle McLymont, principal of McLymont, Kunda & Co. of Valley Cottage, NY and Jamaica.

5 The source is Reggie Twigg, ERP Market Specialist for Printonix of Irvine, California.

6 Mik Chwalek, a former partner in Coopers & Lybrand's Knowledge Strategies group, quoted in the author's *Supply Chain Survival Kit*, A–Z International, Amherst, MA. © 1999.

7 Company sources are Mike VandenBergh, Director of Business and Trade Development for the port of San Diego; and Dennis Kelly, Vice President of US Ports and Terminals for Dole Food Co. Quoted in "The Best of the Bunch" by Lara L. Sowinski, *World Trade* magazine, August 2001.

The State of the Art

Supply chain theory is always evolving, as is the technology driving the practice. So what are today's hot topics in supply chain management? This chapter explores current trends:

» the move from a supply chain to a supply network;
» the need for improvement on the IT front;
» evolving Web business models; and
» the menace of e-commerce fraud.

''Most distribution channels over the last 50 years have become fragmented and fractured. This significantly inhibits communication flow, and that, in turn, creates tremendous inefficiencies at all stages along that supply chain. The Internet allows real-time communications along the entire supply chain. When coupled with business applications, this begins to squeeze out inefficiencies and increase productivity.''

Walter W. Buckley III,[1] *co-founder, President, and CEO, Internet Capital Group*

INTRODUCTION

As we enter a new phase of supply chain management – the Web-enabled world that will aid the evolution of a supply network – there are many issues to be resolved. The dot-com mania that swept the world for several years, ending in the fall of 2000, taught many companies that they need to continue to focus on sensible business planning and to consider technology a tool, not a panacea. Since that time there has been a call to get back to basics, and that means applying sensible approaches to supply chain management that date back a decade or more.

Supply chain theorists are currently debating the role of forecasting as it relates to the supply chain.

''Some true believers are arguing that supply chain theory carried to its logical conclusion can effectively eliminate the need for forecasting. Others believe there will always be a need to predict consumer behavior and the vagaries that can influence preferences. It's from the forecast the rest of the chain can plan its demand; what's called demand planning.''[2]

While the theorists debate the future of forecasting, companies and institutions face the issue of assessing what technology makes sense to implant and gearing up for a world that will certainly be networked and Web-enabled. You have to be able to operate a supply chain with whatever technology is available now while always keeping an eye out to adapt to technology trends that make sense.

For example, the Web is well suited to procurement and some forms of sourcing, so prepare your organization to practice e-procurement and e-sourcing. If it's economically feasible to move to an online logistics approach through a third-party vendor, and that approach means cost savings for your organization, then there's no reason not to move in that direction. Technology, and dot-coms, are here to stay even if they don't take the shape of the pioneers that emerged in the early part of this century.

But with the move to the Web, particularly the emergence of capabilities that allow global sourcing and purchasing online, come very real issues of security, fraud, and the need to understand the laws and regulations of the markets you are entering throughout the world. These are just some among the array of issues that supply chain experts are studying and debating.

MOVING FROM A SUPPLY CHAIN TO A SUPPLY NETWORK

While the so-called "Global 2000" companies are already forming collaborative trading groups (see below), many other companies are still operating with phone, fax, and perhaps a dedicated e-mail line. In the next decade, or even sooner, these organizations will have to consider moving to a networked, Web-enabled world to survive. The following are areas in which changes need to be considered when making the switch from a supply chain to working in a supply network:

» internal communication;
» business process communication;
» external communication;
» computing;
» procurement;
» inventory management;
» shipping.

See Chapter 4 for more details.

EVOLUTION OF COLLABORATIVE GROUPS

Major companies, from Wal-Mart to Ford Motor Co., IBM to Sears, Roebuck and Co., are all upgrading their core systems to take full advantage of the Internet/Web. Many of the Global 2000 companies are also creating private, collaborative supply communities and forcing their supply chain channel partners to follow suit. They are practicing what is called "business-to-business" (B2B) electronic commerce or the real-time flow of information between partners or real-time online business transactions.

B2B offers many benefits, of which potential savings is considered just one. Moving into a collaborative B2B approach allows for better planning and execution – both upstream and downstream in the supply chain – which in turn affects costs. That is planning as it relates to almost all facets of manufacturing and distribution, including design, forecasting, procurement, production and fulfillment, logistics, order management, change orders, and channel management. The aim is to remove process inefficiencies, improve inventory management, free up working capital, and generally improve productivity and cut costs.

> "Increasingly, manufacturers and suppliers are becoming one enterprise ... With supply chain management, the sales-order system of the buying company becomes at one with the purchase-order system of the selling company. It drives the concept of synchronization across partners in the supply chain ... The goal is the transformation of linear, serial supply chains into parallel, collaborative communities, dramatically reducing cycle times, improving customer relationships, and increasing productivity."[3]

ROOM FOR IMPROVEMENT ON THE IT FRONT

Experts are finding that global e-commerce continues to fuel sales of global logistics solutions software, and the market is poised for further growth if software suppliers can produce improved solutions desired by international shippers.

That is the conclusion of a recent study conducted by ARC, a Dedham, MA, based consulting firm, which indicated a need for major improvements before global logistics solutions can really meet the tougher demands of a global economy. In particular, the study urges global logistics software be connected to other business applications. Shippers will no longer be satisfied with the ability to simply track shipments.

> "At a minimum, the study recommends, software providers should have a team of trade experts on staff to provide basic consulting and support services. These could cover product classification, workflow design and international trade education. Most important, for complex consulting projects such as designing a global supply-chain network, the providers should establish partnerships with consulting firms that specialize in this type of work."[4]

EVOLVING WEB BUSINESS MODELS

The world of Web-enabled purchasing, with marketplaces, exchanges, and auctions, is still evolving. The advantages of being able to scour the world for the best goods at the price sounds great in theory, but is not always great in practice. As procurement experts point out, price is not the only condition that makes a sale worthwhile. There are issues of trust and sheer logistics that come into play. If goods from China are cheaper, but the supplier is unknown and the shipping costs exorbitant, that supplier with the higher cost who is in your neighborhood may seem more appealing.

And as companies experiment with emerging Web models, some are emerging as more viable than others. Both Amazon.com and eBay earned praise for developing smart business models and for surviving the dot-com crash of 2000/2001. Studies that were published in 2001 indicate that other Web practices – online reverse auctions – may not be the way to go. According to research conducted at the Massachusetts Institute of Technology's Sloan School of Management, online reverse auctions can damage relationships between buyers and suppliers. Sealed-bid auctions, on the other hand, appear to be less damaging to the buyer/supplier relationship.

> "Suppliers who took part in the open-bid process 'felt exploited.' They felt the relationship between supplier and buyer had been severed, and that they had been 'forced into an online arena

where they would battle it out with each other, leading to reduced price'."[5]

The sealed-bid process proved more satisfactory to suppliers, according to the MIT study. There was more opportunity to build a relationship between buyer and seller and to work towards ongoing business, rather than a one-time sales opportunity. The study concludes:

> "Online reverse auctions can bring reduced prices for buyers, but they should be used sparingly, and only for certain types of goods. Buyers should use online auctions when they feel the need to weed out non-competitive suppliers."

COMBATING E-COMMERCE FRAUD

There are many forms of e-commerce fraud. Hackers can cause major trouble by accessing confidential information or actually shutting down networks. Ascertaining who is legitimate while functioning in cyberspace is a major concern for service providers and customers alike.

» For the service provider, getting paid is a real problem – particularly when operating internationally – and outsourcing in cyberspace presents its own risks to your supply chain.
» The customer worries about international transactions being legitimate.

Transport and logistics dot-coms are all gearing up to protect themselves and their customers. From establishing *firewalls*, to tracing purchaser identities, conducting Dunn & Bradstreet checks, credit checks and constant vigilance, they are all working to keep business on the Web clean.

Setting up Web security is a first step for most of these companies. Calling complacency "the biggest fear" and physical security "the biggest risk," they are surrounding themselves with the appropriate firewalls. Some dot-coms conduct audits against that information to make sure that what goes through is indeed a valid business type of electronic fax. Issuing IDs is a major way of protecting Websites from cyber-terrorists.[6]

NOTES

1 Quoted in "Supply chain management: back to basics" by John Ince, *Upside Media*, June 4 2001 – reprinted in *Supply Strategy*, online edn, May/June 2001.

2 Dr John T. Mentzer, Bruce Chair of Excellence in Business, Department of Marketing, Logistics and Transportation, University of Tennessee.

3 "Supply chain management: back to basics" by John Ince; see note 1.

4 "Global logistics systems aren't up to par," *Supply Strategy*, online edn, May/June 2001.

5 "Negotiating: auctions alienate key suppliers, research shows" by Sandy Jap, Professor of Marketing, MIT, *Supply Strategy*, online edn, May/June 2001.

6 For further discussion, see "Someone out there wants to cheat you!" by Amy Zuckerman, *World Trade* magazine, March 2001, pp. 36–38.

Success Stories in Practice

What are the secrets of creating a great supply chain? This chapter explores how Compaq, Fujitsu PC and Staples have managed to success-fully employ supply chain management for competitive advantage. It includes:

» a case study of Compaq's forward, pre-position model;
» a case study of Fujitsu PC's transport/logistics reorganization; and
» a case study of Staples' European organization launch.

This chapter looks at three case studies involving:

» computer manufacturer and vendor Compaq and third-party logistics company CTI;
» a partnership between Fujitsu and Federal Express; and
» a European operation for Staples, the office products retailer.

COMPAQ[1]

"The primary focus of this program has been to free up working capital from the standpoint of postponed procurement, and we've been very successful in doing that. In the past, we used to commit with a supplier beforehand and Compaq paid for the material on receiving it into the warehouse. Right now a supplier is ostensibly lending their materials and aren't paid until those materials are pulled."

Mark Morrison,[2] Vice President, Business Development, Customized Transportation Inc.

The set-up

In the space of several years, computer manufacturer and vendor Compaq has moved from a traditional inventory model where components were paid and warehoused in anticipation of manufacturing, to a forward or pre-position model which allows for just-in-time shipping and manufacturing.

Following the example of Dell, which championed the forward materials approach, the Houston-based computer giant has been able to promote speedy, accurate and on-time shipments from its network of 200 global suppliers. In the process, Compaq has slashed "millions in working capital," according to Customized Transportation Inc. (CTI) of Jacksonville, Florida, which manages the inbound manufacturing materials flow for Compaq's Houston assembly plant.[3]

Like many companies, Compaq used to maintain several sites where they stored and positioned materials to meet their manufacturing requirements. That meant heavy up-front costs, as the computer company used to operate on a "purchase and place" basis and supplier/vendors were paid up-front. CTI was hired to develop a forward or pre-positioning system where the terms of sale don't take place until the materials are actually pulled into manufacture from the vendor. CTI was able to implement a vendor-managed system over an 18–24-month period starting in 1998 when it set up its Houston materials center.

Compaq manufactures product seven days a week, 24 hours a day – "24 by 7" in manufacturing lingo – almost every day of the year. Manufacturing sites are down three to four days a year, if that. About 60–70% of its parts and components come from offshore, with the Pacific Rim being the most significant supplier.

CTI's relationship with Compaq does not end with the redesign of its supply chain flow. The third-party logistics company has also entered this high-paced, high-tension mix by acting as the suppliers' manager in what is described as a "triangular relationship." Suppliers that conduct business with Compaq agree to execute a contract with CTI to manage their materials. About 95% of suppliers take advantage of these services rather than installing their own "bricks and mortar" logistics site in Houston, which is what Compaq requires of those outside the CTI fold. Although CTI manages the actual material flow from most of its suppliers, it is Compaq that maintains the business relationship. Whether it is billing or setting up terms for stock replenishment, that comes from Compaq.

> "The savings figure is true. What it comes down to is that with this system of supplier-owned inventory at the hub, inventory is positioned at CTI's center and basically isn't on Compaq's books. Before we had the relationship with CTI we had to take receivership and ownership of the materials that went into our books."[4]

This same system is now in place and functional at Compaq's Scotland and Singapore manufacturing operations. However, two different third-party logistics providers handle those accounts.

Moving materials to Houston

Compaq's Houston manufacturing operation is its largest worldwide. Products assembled in Houston are of the "bread-and-butter" server line – the big line of servers that support all of the electronic commerce industry today, as well as personal computers including laptops and PCs. The company also maintains assembly and manufacturing sites in Scotland, and in Pacific Rim nations such as Singapore and China.

CTI maintains separate contracts with 200 or so of Compaq's world-wide suppliers. All told, they produce and ship to Houston over 6000 parts used in the manufacturing process. To do this, CTI maintains a 410,000-square-foot automated warehousing facility located within 15 minutes of the Compaq assembly plant, so it can quickly and efficiently receive, store, and ship materials as the manufacturer needs them.

Here's a step-by-step scenario of how CTI, the supply base and Compaq coordinate in-bound shipments and the warehouse replenishment that follows. This example is based on what a large-scale customer in Compaq's Major Accounts Direct would experience:

1 A multinational company orders 1000 desktop computers. To fulfill that order, Compaq needs to aggregate production materials.
2 The order for individual finished units is defined in a bill of materials (BOM) that offers a complete, detailed breakout of all the components necessary to manufacturer the unit ordered.
3 The BOM is transmitted through standard electronic data interchange (EDI) to CTI's Houston materials center and received into their inventory control system. Utilizing a modified version of the software program Catalyst, the system is able to translate the BOM and designate the quantities of materials required to meet manufacturing schedules.
4 From the time CTI receives the bill of materials, the logistics operation has four hours or so to pick all materials and ship them to Compaq's plant where cellular manufacturing stations will build each computer system ordered. All materials will be used during this process simultaneously, so shipments from the Houston materials center take place all at once.
5 To make this happen at top speed, the order is broken down by the CTI computer system to produce pick instructions for warehouse workers. Orders are delivered electronically right to the warehouse handling equipment and include instructions on the most efficient moves to make through the warehouse to avoid unnecessary steps. Pickers, armed with RF (radio-frequency) equipment, then collect or pick all materials listed for shipment.

6 Once the picking is completed, there are approximately a dozen destinations within Compaq where material is delivered. CTI maintains a shuttle between its materials center and the Compaq assembly plant every hour on the hour.

7 Once the shipment arrives at Compaq, they send an EDI message back to the CTI materials center advising them of its safe arrival. Simultaneously, Compaq alerts all suppliers involved in the shipment that their materials have been pulled. This announcement includes an invoice to the suppliers from Compaq.

Replenishment and the relationship with global suppliers

A great deal of what makes the forward positioning model possible is electronic access to all information available on a supplier's materials and shipment. Imagine a global community of over 200 suppliers that have to have "24-by-7" access to the movements of inventory that's received and docked in Houston and then delivered to Compaq. CTI handles this problem by providing Web access to their inventory system.

Compaq, in turn, has a process whereby they project manufacturing needs for one business quarter and then relay their manufacturing requirements to their supply base via EDI. The supply base then commits to those requirements in terms of moving the materials to the warehouse. CTI is not engaged in that activity directly. Replenishment is the function of the advanced shipment notice from Compaq to EDI-capable suppliers.

> "An Asian supplier can dial into our inventory system via the Web and see what's occurred over the last day, week or quarter in terms of the status of their materials. They can monitor their materials as they're pulled from inventory whether they're from South America, the Pacific Rim or elsewhere. Suppliers are asked to position so much material at the hub. Procurement makes sure those lines are met."[5]

Suppliers to Houston from Brazil, France, Scotland, and China are also part of a plant-to-plant network that allows Compaq to shift materials to various manufacturing operations depending on production needs.

CTI officials call this process "inventory balancing." If Compaq has shortages from one operation and over-capacity in another, CTI serves as a conduit to balance inventories.

CTI also offers ancillary services to Compaq's global supply community. For example, foreign suppliers might ask the logistics company to handle product inspections or tests required by the US government. If the materials are rejected, then CTI will sort them and move them back through the supply chain.

Benefits of forward positioning

CTI officials believe the forward positioning model is working well for Compaq. Besides making the supply chain transparent for both customers and suppliers, they believe the savings this system promotes have been very real. If there has been any major adjustment from the company's standpoint, it is that the Compaq manufacturing units now handle the supplier invoicing that used to be the purview of the Compaq warehousing operations.

The program has been particularly strong in freeing up working capital from the standpoint of postponed procurement. The past system has been abolished where a commitment with a supplier is made beforehand and Compaq paid for the material on receiving it into the warehouse. Right now a supplier is ostensibly lending their materials and are not paid until those materials are pulled.

Suppliers benefit as well, they say, because of the transparency of the system. Offering suppliers Web access so they can track their own materials and know when to replenish has been a key concern of both Compaq and CTI.

"The reason the Web visibility is so important is that the access to information is as important as the movement of materials. If you were dealing in a paper or fax environment, you couldn't do this. And that's where we were several years ago."[6]

TIME LINE

From 1998 to 2000, Compaq Computers teamed with Customized Transportation Inc. to set up both a forward-positioning logistics center in Houston and a forward-positioning, just-in-time model with suppliers. This process was accomplished over a period of 18-24 months.

KEY INSIGHTS

» Just-in-time systems pay off handsomely in terms of reduced inventory costs.

» Logistics outsourcing can work for manufacturers with the right communication flow from all parties, arrangements with suppliers, and process transparency.

» There must be full cooperation from all supply chain partners and a trusting relationship between the manufacturer and 3PL.

» Providing process transparency on the Web has paid off so that all suppliers - regional and global - have constant access to shipment and inventory information.

A FUJITSU AND FEDERAL EXPRESS PARTNERSHIP[7]

"The difference has been huge. We set a goal that by the end of 1998 we would be competitive in our performance on order fulfillment and by March of 1999 we would be world-class. Now, our reliability-of-delivery performance is above 95 percent, while some of our competitors are in the high 80s and proud of it. Our shipping accuracy is above 98 percent, and the accuracy of last week's cycle count of inventory was 100 percent."

Bruce Anderson,[8] Vice President of Operations, Fujitsu PC - a subsidiary of Fujitsu Corporation

The background

Outsourcing its logistics operation to Federal Express (FedEx) has worked for Fujitsu PC, but not without a lot of tweaking. In 1997, Fujitsu PC, with a US base in Milpitas, California, needed help with its notebook operation, which was suffering from both excess inventory and slow deliveries. Despite high inventories, it took 10 days to get a notebook to a customer.

Most components assembled in the US came from suppliers in Japan and were shipped to a manufacturing and assembly plant in Portland, Oregon. Circle Air Freight handled the inbound transit and Nippon Express handled the Japanese end. Finished products were stored in a warehouse facility and then shipped outbound to US sales channels through FedEx and United Parcel Service (UPS).

Problems centered on the inbound end. For example, large shipments destined for Portland would show up in Oakland or somewhere else. Fujitsu PC officials cited a lack of visibility, control, and consistency to shipment performance that was tied to a lack of coordination and clear-cut responsibility between the two freight forwarders.

"There were too many people involved on the forwarder end and there was too little control from Fujitsu, and the whole process served to increase our freight cost, delay our response to customers, and make much more confusing a lot of the logistical elements of new product introductions. In turn, this delayed the customer's service level, delayed our time to market, and ultimately was costing us considerable amounts of money."[9]

In the winter/spring of 1998, the Japanese company turned to FDX Corp. – parent company of FedEx – for a total logistics solution. Officials recognized that Portland was not a good hub for servicing the continental US and saw outsourcing as a solution to its supply chain woes. FDX Corp. was providing total logistics services from its Memphis distribution center to several well-known high-tech customers and seemed right for the job. Fujitsu PC officials liked the FedEx operation and the proximity to Memphis-area manufacturing subcontractors with experience providing overnight technical services for electronics testing, assembly, and repair.

Fujitsu PC's goals in hiring FedEx were to increase customer choice, and to try to get a 25-day customer response time from first call to product delivery down to an average of four days. That meant reducing response time by a factor of five to six, requiring examination of the entire physical layout of their worldwide network, including interfacing with customers and the technology at hand.

Huge planning before making the switch

"As an organization, it required us to work on a global basis not only with Fujitsu PC but with the parent company in Japan and with Asian suppliers as well. Since we were bringing a total solution, it required a cross-section of functional areas of our company, such as information technology, billing and legal."[10]

A huge amount of effort went into mapping the physical flow of material. Fujitsu PC was seeking flawless execution that depended on early electronic commerce capabilities. They understood the crucial need for information to move smoothly and in a timely manner, for money to be in the right accounts at the right time, and the need to meet import/export regulations.

As the time neared to shift the assembly and shipping operation to Memphis, many issues emerged, including instituting an anti-theft process at the FedEx facility. It's one thing to protect large servers that cannot be lifted, but notebooks are light and easy to steal. Importing Fujitsu PC's Oracle enterprise resource planning (ERP) system into the Memphis warehouse – right down to the shipping dock – proved to be another challenge. Although cost-effective in the long run, it meant that FedEx workers had to be trained in Oracle. Overcoming these issues pushed the start-up schedule into early fall of 1998. And Fujitsu PC found that it had to keep its customer base constantly apprised of the changeover and explain any erratic service.

How the partnership worked

The Fujitsu PC ERP system was centered at the company's headquarters in Milpitas with an electronic link to the FedEx facility in Memphis. The primary architecture was provided by a company called Vitria.

» Inbound parts and components arrived in Memphis from Asian suppliers via FedEx planes and were stored in a FedEx warehouse facility. Orders were received into the Milpitas Oracle system, which took the data and ran its MRP (materials resource planning) program.

» Production schedules were passed electronically from Milpitas to another FedEx facility in Memphis that housed the company's so-called "integrated repair and return" (IRR) operation as well as to a separate Fujitsu PC operation housed about two miles away and staffed with Fujitsu PC employees.

» In a designated space connected to the IRR by a separate tunnel, a subcontractor provided the technicians and capability to assemble and test the notebooks. Similar assembly, software loading, testing, and some refurbishing activity was performed also at the other facility in Memphis by Fujitsu PC employees.

» Milpitas assigned tasks and product lines individually to each facility depending on volume demands and order patterns. A master scheduler on the Oracle system in Milpitas moved orders into the appropriate assembly queue once the orders had been cleared by other administrative elements within the Oracle package.

» At the IRR in Memphis, workers pulled the day's orders off the Oracle system and processed them, sending instructions to the FedEx warehouse as to what parts and components were needed. These parts and components were shuttled to the IRR and to the off-site Fujitsu PC operation. Technicians at both facilities assembled the day's orders and packaged the notebooks for outbound transport.

» Receiving transactions, shipping transactions, and changes to inventory data were made directly into the Oracle system in Memphis and uploaded to the mainframe.

Results

Information was integrated very closely into the Oracle system, which allowed Fujitsu PC to provide direct input to FedEx about what shipments were arriving in Memphis and the ability to monitor inventory. In return, the FedEx system provided shipment visibility for all products moving along the supply chain. Once orders were dropped to Memphis, the normal expectation was delivery within three days. That allowed for one-day cycle time through the Memphis assembly operation and the ability to maintain low inventories. The fast turnaround on inventories meant a shorter shelf time and made the parts and components less susceptible to price deterioration.

Fujitsu PC also plugged into FedEx's proof-of-delivery system, so the computer manufacturer's accounts-receivable department received immediate electronic copies of signed proof-of-delivery forms, which enabled prompt billing.

Despite the headaches, by 1999 Fujitsu PC was reaping the benefits of its alliance. There was:

"... a tremendous decrease in the total cost of logistics. For example, return and refurbish expenses have been reduced significantly, and finished goods inventory has been reduced by about 90 percent due to the speed and reliability of the pipelines from Asia and through Memphis. When I arrived here, there were 22,000 units in inventory. We now have fewer than 2,000 either finished or under construction ... We also dramatically reduced our channel inventory. Now we are in total control of our shipping in such a way that we can prevent the unnecessary build-up in the pipeline of inbound parts and components."[11]

By June of 1999, Fujitsu PC was able to start moving its supply chain onto the Web and sell directly to customers. With Web business to individuals and companies picking up, they started eliminating distributors and establishing direct connection with a small number of valued-added resellers and select retailers to bolster their Web channel. Other Web opportunities were being explored at this writing, with the recognition that, although the Web can promote direct sales, they have to be supported by hands-on shipping and delivery.

"A consumer only spends ten minutes ordering this complex device on the Web, then has to wait around all morning for someone to come by and deliver it. Clearly there's a mismatch of capabilities at work here. In these days of cell phones, you would think that things would be easier."[12]

TIME LINE
- » **1997**: Fujitsu PC recognizes it must address its shipping/delivery/inventory problem.
- » **Winter 1998**: The company selects FedEx to outsource its entire logistics operation.
- » **Spring 1998**: A contract is signed.

> » **Summer/fall**: Major glitches relating to security and IT are sorted out, while the company juggles with ongoing customer demand.
> » **Fall 1998**: FedEx's Memphis operation takes over Fujitsu PC logistics.
> » **Winter/spring 1999**: The partners start exploring a Web presence.

KEY INSIGHTS

> » Do not ignore the transport side of the supply chain. When shipments are delayed, the supply chain breaks down.
> » Pick your logistics outsourcing partner with tremendous care.
> » Make certain this partner has the IT and security measures required for an electronic/Web-enabled approach to logistics.
> » Integrate all business processes for maximum cost-containment. Make sure your system is compatible with alliance partners.

STAPLES' EUROPEAN OPERATION[13]

"Europe is totally different [from the US]. That's the reason why we installed a European management team."

Luc Bosems,[14] *Manager, Distribution Center, Tongeren,*
Belgium

The background

Second only to Office Depot, Framingham, MA-based Staples is the second-largest office products superstore retailer in the US, maintaining about 1200 stores at this writing. In recent years, its aim was to aggressively boost sales and market share in Europe with the goal of 20% growth in sales, and 25–30% growth in profits. The plan was to meet these goals by increasing the number of office-supply stores, catalog orders, contract stationery business, and Internet retailing. The challenge was to balance growth while maintaining a multichannel, transatlantic supply chain and duplicating Staples' US success while taking into consideration the unique European market.

Although Europe likes to promote itself as a common market, the reality is quite different. Companies doing business in the EU still confront a myriad of European national regulations that sit alongside EU regulations (called Directives), labeling and packaging requirements, local languages, a variety of sale tax regimes, and environmental restrictions. As it prepared to launch a European operation, Staples had to confront all of those issues and more, including cultural differences. Recognizing that Europe is not the US, a European management team was established right from the start.

In the fall of 2000, the company opened European headquarters, a distribution center, and a call center in three locations throughout Belgium. The country was picked not because Staples planned to do business in Belgium, but rather for its central location. Company officials point out that 60% of Europe's purchasing power lies within 500 km of Belgium, whose government offered the company tax breaks to locate there. The catalog business was housed just outside Brussels; the distribution center 50 miles east in Tongeren near the Dutch and German borders, and the call center in Eupen in Walloonia.[15]

Within a short time the company had established 165 retail outlets on the continent; 50 in Germany, 70 in the United Kingdom, with the rest scattered throughout the Netherlands and Portugal. By the end of 2001, Staples expected to have opened operations in the Netherlands and possibly France.

Meeting logistics challenges

All this growth necessitated expanding the catalog arm and strengthening the new European management structure. It also meant ensuring quick delivery of goods from vendors to meet Staples' promise of next-day delivery to catalog customers who order by 6 pm in most countries. Officials knew that in time the Tongeren distribution center would not be sufficient and they might have to duplicate these efforts closer to customers in other countries. They expected the Tongeren center – with 12,000 square meters – to be able to handle European volume for four to five years. At its opening, only 20–50% of the space was being utilized and there was room at this location to handle twice the volume and add about 100 employees to the current 50.

Throughout 2000 and into 2001, the company maintained a conservative approach to opening new distribution facilities, planning new sites as it moved into new regions. For example, the overseas catalog business was restricted to customers in Germany and the UK, with one distribution center allocated for each.

While studying the possibility of setting up centralized delivery to retail outlets in Europe, Staples officials decided to maintain separate supply chains for each. Shipments to stores came mostly directly from vendors while the catalog business was supported from the Tongeren distribution center. The concern was developing an integrated marketing perspective and sales channels. The European call center in Walloonia had about 50 agents and was expected to expand to more than 300. Plans were made to include multilingual staff and to expand the number of call centers as growth in Europe warranted.

For automated tracking of products, Staples' European operation relied on a warehouse management system from GDA. The system keeps track of product location within the warehouse, generating replenishment alerts when needed. Outbound shipments are prepared according to daily pick lists. Staffers have also instituted a color-coding system to back up IT efforts. Shipments are color-coded by the day for easy sorting.

Moving to an online approach

Before moving to Web sales, Staples officials worked on instituting common practices throughout the European sales operation, along with building a coherent brand identity in the minds of customers. Finding cooperation points between the catalog and retail businesses was also a goal. As in the US, shoppers who fail to find a product in stores were encouraged to consult the catalog, which offered a wider selection.

The next step was developing Internet sales similar to the Staples.com operation in place in the US and Canada since 1998. The company was laying the organizational groundwork for the dot-com channel at this writing, with hopes of a launch in the fall of 2001. Internet sales were expected to broaden product offerings to 200,000 items, as compared with the 20,000 items offered in the catalog and 7000 items available in retail outlets.

Besides increasing sales, the Internet was seen as a vehicle for promoting improved electronic links between Staples Europe and its suppliers. A standardized system for merchandising and back-office functions was already in place. But to meet dot-com sales demand, Staples was building a data warehouse that would secondarily offer additional electronic information flow to suppliers.

Even so, the dot-com launch posed challenges. Company officials were concerned that the dot-com should not cannibalize other divisions. They wanted the catalog, retail, and dot-com operations to coexist to meet customer demand, not compete with each other. The plan at this writing was to funnel dot-com business through the catalog distribution centers, which would have the additional benefit of best utilizing European warehouses.

Whether to open another line – a version of the US Stapleslink.com – was on the drawing board at this writing. Stapleslink.com allows the company to act as an office-supply manager on behalf of business customers. European company officials were holding off on this option for the time being.

High costs, high marks

Although Germany was providing the highest sales potential, it was also one of the most costly countries in which to do business. Staples Europe was finding that smaller markets in Scandinavia and the Benelux countries were yielding higher returns. High real-estate costs in Germany and other concerns led company officials to close the Hamburg warehouse and begin serving German catalog customers from Tongeren.

Despite these issues, analysts give Staples Europe high marks for organization and efficiency. Analysts studying the European operation believe that the company's combination of retail and direct merchandizing are good ways of maximizing its distribution network. And they praise the decision to rely on centralized distribution, which competitors like Office Depot and OfficeMax are just starting to embrace.

Staples also garners analyst praise for the way it handled its dot-com operation, using the Internet as a growth channel without disrupting its bricks-and-mortar operation. Staples Europe seems poised to benefit from Internet sales, and the dot-com will permit continued growth.[16]

TIME LINE

- » **Fall 2000**: Staples Europe opens a headquarters, distribution center, and call center in three locations in Belgium.
- » **Fall 2000-spring 2001**: Within a short time the company has established 165 retail outlets on the continent; 50 in Germany, and 70 in the UK, with the rest scattered throughout the Netherlands and Portugal. The company closes a Hamburg distribution center because of costs, and holds off from opening additional centers.
- » **Remainder of 2001**: The dot-com division is expected to launch in the fall of 2001. Operations are slated for opening in the Netherlands and possibly France by the end of 2001.

KEY INSIGHTS

- » The European market is still highly fragmented and requires specialized management with knowledge of local customs, languages and regulations.
- » Centralized distribution pays off in efficiencies and cost savings.
- » Careful upfront planning pays off followed by conservative growth.
- » The costs of doing business in Europe are deceptive. Profits can be eaten away by high real-estate costs and taxes.
- » It is important to establish common operating practices – particularly sales – throughout the European operation, while allowing for a variety of approaches to match individual national cultures.
- » All divisions – retail sales, catalogs, and dot-com – must complement each other, not compete and cannibalize each other.

NOTES

1 Case study adapted from "Compaq switches to pre-position inventory model" by Amy Zuckerman, *World Trade* magazine, April 2000.

2 Quoted in "Compaq switches to pre-position inventory model" by Amy Zuckerman; *ibid*.

3 *Ibid*.

4 Bill Moore, material logistics manager for Compaq's Houston manufacturing operation; *ibid*.

5 *Ibid*.

6 Mark Morrison, vice president, business development, Customized Transportation Inc.; *Ibid*.

7 Case study adapted from "Fujitsu partners with FedEx to boost performance of notebook business" by Kurt C. Hoffman, *Global Logistics & Supply Chain Strategies*, online edn, November 1999.

8 Quoted in "Fujitsu partners with FedEx to boost performance of notebook business" by Kurt C. Hoffman; *ibid*.

9 Bruce Anderson, vice president of operations, Fujitsu PC; *ibid*.

10 Brent Meyers, then managing director of sales for FedEx's electronic commerce unit; *ibid*.

11 See note 9.

12 See note 9.

13 Case study adapted from "Increased European sales for Staples? Yeah, We've Got That" by Robert J. Bowman, *Global Logistics & Supply Chain Strategies*, online edn, February, 2001.

14 Quoted in "Increased European sales for Staples? Yeah, We've got that" by Robert J. Bowman; *ibid*.

15 Jo Verbeek, vice president of operations for the catalog business of Staples Inc. in Europe and Luc Bosems; *ibid*.

16 Mark Mandel, senior vice president, Robinson-Humphrey Co. Inc., New York, NY; *ibid*.

Key Concepts and Players

Supply chain theory and practice has its own lingo and key players promoting the field. Get to grips with the lexicon of supply chain with the ExpressExec supply chain glossary in this chapter.

"Management is on the verge of a major breakthrough in understanding how industrial company success depends on the interactions between the flows of information, materials, money, manpower and capital equipment."

Jay W. Forrester[1]

A GLOSSARY FOR SUPPLY CHAIN MANAGEMENT

The author acknowledges the following for inspiration for many of the items in this glossary: John T. Mentzer (ed.), *Supply Chain Management*, Sage Publications Inc.

Area planner purchasing approach – an approach ulitizing a centralized purchasing group, responsible for suppliers, while field production and logistics planners manage the actual operating flows between firms.

Automatic replenishment – systems used to replenish inventory automatically by giving suppliers the right to anticipate future requirements, thereby reducing inventory and increasing availability.

Channel of distribution – a set of companies with the collective ability to intensively distribute materials and products to selected target markets and/or extensively distribute to wide geographical areas and/or market segments.

Cross-docking – a process where incoming shipments are transferred into an outgoing shipment without entering the warehouse.

Decision support systems (DSS) – interactive, computer-based systems that provide data and analysis and analytic models to help decision-makers solve unstructured problems.

Efficient consumer response (ECR) – originating in the grocery industry, ECR aims to replenish inventory based on real-time sales data obtained from point-of-sale information that is transmitted back through the supply chain.

Electronic data interchange (EDI) – standardized electronic transmission formats for large-scale data transmission on private computer networks.

Enterprise resource planning (ERP) – both a practice and form of software solution used to integrate back-office practices.

Forecasting performance measurement – the availability and application of forecasting performance measures, including four dimensions: measurement challenge, measurement clarity, measurement criteria, and measurement feedback.

Just-in-time (JIT) – manufacturing is geared to production upon orders, not based on inventorying.

Logistics – the combination of warehousing and shipping.

Materials resource planning (or materials requirements planning – MRP) – managing the supply side of a firm by computing net requirements for each inventory item to schedule production, and determining when they should be purchased and delivered to the plant to minimize inventory, transportation costs, and warehousing requirements.

Supply chain – a set of three or more companies directly linked by one or more of the upstream and downstream flows of products, services, finances, and information from a source to a customer.

KEY PLAYERS

Introduction

Supply chain management is both a management theory that is constantly evolving and being taught in business schools globally, and an ongoing industry practice. Literally hundreds of books and thousands of articles have been written on the subject over the last decade or so. Contributions to both the theory and the practice have been made by academics and industry, and often by the combined forces of both.

As noted particularly in Chapter 3, there are a number of factors that make up a supply chain, and therefore a number of avenues of theory and practice. Some supply chain experts are truly experts in procurement, others in marketing. There are others who specialize in logistics and transportation. Supply chain experts may be those who study manufacturing cycles. Yet others have expertise in technology and how it affects the supply chain.

It is impossible to mention here all those individuals who have contributed to the advancement of supply chain theory and practice. Because of the enormity of the field, it is also difficult to list some key players in this arena and not others. Unlike the quality field, where certain individuals have taken on guru status and enjoy almost household name recognition, the supply chain has evolved thanks to the efforts of many brilliant men and women.

Editors of supply chain journals and practitioners were asked to identify those members of the supply chain community who have made seminal contributions to the field. The following contains their recommendations of individuals who are considered key players in this arena, introduced alphabetically. They range from specialists in marketing to manufacturing, logistics, order processing, and transportation, along with others, but in no way constitute the entire breadth of qualified individuals.

Rick D. Blasgen

Rick Blasgen is a 1983 graduate of Governor's State University with a degree in Business Administration and was a finance major. He began his career with Nabisco Inc. in a regional customer service center in Chicago. There he held various logistics positions in inventory management, order processing, transportation; and he supervised a distribution center operation. He is currently Vice-President, Supply Chain.

Mr Blasgen transferred to Virginia in 1987 as manager of Nabisco's private distribution center in Chesapeake, VA. In 1988, he moved to Pennsylvania and spent four years as Eastern Region Operations Manager. In August 1992, he moved to Nabisco's headquarters in New Jersey where he was Director of Operations until June 1993, when he became Director of National Inventory Management. In August 1996, he was appointed Senior Director, Product Supply, and became Vice-President, Supply Chain in June 1998.

He spends much of his time furthering Nabisco's company-wide supply chain management programs and initiatives.

Mr Blasgen is a member of the executive committee of the Council of Logistics Management and a Past President of the Warehousing Education and Research Council. He is also a member of the logistics/distribution committee of the Grocery Manufacturers of America and on the Editorial Advisory Board for the International Journal of Physical Distribution and Logistics Management.

Dr Donald J. Bowersox

Donald Bowersox is currently Dean of the Eli Broad College of Business and is the John H. McConnell University Professor of Business Administration at the Eli Broad Graduate School of Management at Michigan State University. During his career, Dean Bowersox has served as an air force pilot and in various business capacities, including Vice President and General Manager of the E.F. MacDonald Company. He currently serves on the Strategy Advisory Board of AmeriCold Logistics, A.T. Kearney's GEO-Award Global Review Board, and the Board of Directors, GSC Mobile Solutions.

Dean Bowersox has over 30 years of experience as a consultant to business and government. He frequently presents at professional meetings, such as Efficient Consumer Response (ECR) Initiative, Grocery Manufacturers of America, the Food Marketing Institute, the International Mass Retail Association, the National Electronic Distributors Association, and the Pharmaceutical Manufacturers Association.

In 1967, he founded and continues to co-direct the annual Michigan State University Logistics Supply Chain Management Executive Seminar. He has lectured and taught logistics internationally in over twenty nations.

Dean Bowersox has authored over 250 articles on marketing, transportation, and logistics. He is author or co-author of 15 books including the first logistics text published. His research focuses on logistics and supply chain management organization and strategy. His most recent book, *21st Century Logistics: Making Supply Chain Integration a Reality*, was published in October 1999 by the Council of Logistics Management. He is a member of the editorial review board of the *International Journal of Logistics Management*, the *Journal of Supply Chain Management*, is Associate Editor of the *Journal of International Marketing*, and Visioning Editor of the *Journal of Business Logistics*.

A founding member and the second president of the Council of Logistics Management, Dean Bowersox is a recipient of the Council's Distinguished Service Award. He was awarded a special commendation by the Society of Logistical Engineers (SOLE) for original publication of *Logistical Management*. He has been recognized by Michigan State University as a Distinguished Faculty Member, as well as a Distinguished Alumni. His overall research initiative received the Richard J. Lewis Quality of Excellence Award. He received the Harry E. Salzberg Honorary Medallion presented by Syracuse University.

Dr David J. Closs

David Closs is the Broad Professor of Logistics in the Department of Marketing and Supply Chain Management at Michigan State University. Following the completion of his bachelor degree in mathematics at Michigan State, he was manager of systems development for Systems Research Inc.

For his doctoral dissertation at Michigan State (completed in 1978), he participated in joint university–industry research to test short-range forecasting alternatives. The dissertation, which included the design, implementation, and validation of the computer model used in the research, was given a special award by the National Council of Physical Distribution Management (now the Council of Logistics Management). During a leave from the Michigan State position, Professor Closs was president and CEO of Dialog Systems Inc., a software and consulting firm which provides consulting and software to support logistics planning and operations.

Professor Closs has been extensively involved in the development and application of computer models and information systems for logistics operations and planning. The computer models have included applications for location analysis, inventory management, forecasting, and routing. The information systems development includes inventory management, forecasting, and transportation applications.

Professor Closs has worked with over 100 of the Fortune 500 corporations in areas involving logistics strategy and systems. His experience has focused on the logistics-related issues in the consumer products, medical and pharmaceutical products, and parts industries. He actively participates in logistics executive development seminars and has presented sessions in North America, South America, Asia, Australia, and Eastern Europe.

His primary research interests include logistics strategy, logistics information systems, and logistics planning techniques. He was one of the principal researchers in a three-year study completed by Michigan State University investigating world-class logistics capabilities.

Professor Closs is an active member in the Council of Logistics Management and is former Editor of the *Journal of Business Logistics*.

Notable publications

Professor Closs is the co-author with Donald Bowersox of *World Class Logistics: The Challenge of Managing Continuous Change* (Council of Logistics Management, 1995). Professor Closs and Dr Bowersox are also the authors of *Logistical Management: The Integrated Supply Chain Perspective* (McGraw-Hill, 1996). In addition, the following articles received awards or major visibility:

» Closs, D.J. & Stank, T.P. (1999) "Designing a cross-functional curriculum for supply chain education at Michigan State University." *Journal of Business Logistics*, spring.
» Closs, D.J. *et al.* (1998) "An empirical comparison of anticipatory and response-based supply chain strategies." *International Journal of Logistics Management*, fall.
» Bowersox, D.J., Closs, D.J. & Hall, C.T. (1998) "Beyond ERP: the storm before the calm." *Supply Chain Management Review*, winter, pp. 28–37.
» Bowersox, D.J. & Closs, D.J. (1997) "Brazilian logistics: a time for transition." *Gettao & Producao*, August, pp. 130–139.
» Clinton, S.R. & Closs, D.J. (1997) "Does logistics really have strategy?" *Journal of Business Logistics*, **18**:1, pp. 19–44.
» Closs, D.J., Goldsby, T.J. & Clinton, S.R. (1997) "Information technology influences on world class logistics capability." *International Journal of Physical Distribution and Logistics Management*, **27**:1, pp. 4–17.

Dr John J. Coyle

John Coyle is Professor of Business Administration and corporate sponsors director of the Center for Logistics Research at Penn State University. He holds a bachelor's degree and master's degree from Penn State, and he earned his doctorate at Indiana University, Bloomington, where he was a US Steel Fellow.

Professor Coyle has written over 100 publications in the areas of transportation and logistics. He has presented papers on these same topics at professional meetings, including the Council of Logistics Management, the American Marketing Association, the National Academy of Sciences, the Transportation Research Forum, and the Southern Marketing Association.

Professor Coyle has played an active role in developing the logistics and transportation program at Penn State since joining the faculty in 1961. At Penn State, he has participated regularly in executive education programs as both a lecturer and faculty director. He has been involved as a lecturer on the Executive Management Program, the National Industrial Distributors Program, and the Materials Management – Physical Distribution Program. He has served as Faculty Director of the Executive Management Program and the Emerging Executives Program.

He has been involved in a major program of instructional innovation involving television taped modules for which he received several teaching awards. The latest edition of the tapes is also being used by several Fortune 500 companies and other universities. Professor Coyle has also consulted and provided in-house educational programs for over 200 companies.

He has received eleven college and university awards for outstanding teaching. His current research focuses on the interfaces between logistics, marketing, and manufacturing with particular emphasis on customer service and channels of distribution. A closely related topic that he is pursuing is reverse channels of distribution and their special logistical problems.

In 1991, Professor Coyle received the Council of Logistics Management's top honor – the Distinguished Service Award. This accolade is emblematic of "an individual who has made a significant contribution to the art and science of logistics."

Notable publications

Professor Coyle is co-author of two best-selling textbooks:

» (with Edward J. Bardi and C. John Langley Jr) *The Management of Business Logistics* (South-Western Casebound, 1996);
» (with Edward J. Bardi and Robert A. Novack) *Transportation* (South-Western Casebound, 2000)

He also has been editor of the *Journal of Business Logistics* since being selected in 1990.

Dr Fred Hewitt

Fred Hewitt was born and educated in England where he gained a BA Honors degree and a PhD, in geography and economic development. He is also professionally qualified in education and computing.

Between 1966 and 1970, he lived in Canada, holding a teaching position at the University of Manitoba. He then returned to the UK as Senior Consultant at the National Computing Centre.

Dr Hewitt subsequently joined Rank Xerox and held various positions in Europe, before moving to the US as Xerox's Vice-President of Worldwide Logistics.

In 1993 he returned to the UK to take up his present position as Head of the Aston Business School, Aston University, where he is responsible for the strategic development of the School in both research and teaching.

He also continues to consult, write and lecture in the areas of benchmarking, business process re-engineering, and supply chain management.

Clifford F. Lynch

Clifford Lynch, President of C.F. Lynch & Associates, Memphis, TN, has been providing management advisory services in logistics since 1993. The first 35 years of his career he was Vice President of Logistics for the Quaker Oats Company and President of Trammell Crow Distribution Corporation.

He attended public schools in Memphis, received his undergraduate degree from the University of Tennessee, and an MBA from the University of Chicago.

Mr. Lynch is a Certified Member of the American Society of Transportation and Logistics and is a member of the Logistics Foundation of America (board of directors); *Journal of Business Logistics* (editorial review board); *International Journal of Physical Distribution and Logistics Management* (editorial review board); *Supply Chain Management Review* (editorial review board), and the Warehousing Education and Research Council.

Mr Lynch is also a member and past president of the Council of Logistics Management and has received numerous awards in the field of logistics. Among them are the CLM Distinguished Service Award; *Traffic Management Magazine* Professional Achievement Award; University of Tennessee Department of Marketing and Transportation Distinguished Alumnus; President's Award for Outstanding Contribution to the American Society of Transportation and Logistics; 1992 Salzberg Memorial Medallion; 1997 AST&L Outstanding Transportation/Logistics Executive, and 2000 AST&L Chairman's Award of Excellence.

Notable publications

Clifford Lynch is the author of numerous articles on the subject of logistics. He recently published a book, *Logistics Outsourcing: A Management Guide* (Council of Logistics Management, 2000).

Dr John Thomas (Tom) Mentzer

John Mentzer received his bachelor's degree in 1974 from General Motors Institute, his MBA degree in 1975 from Michigan State University, and his PhD in business, majoring in marketing and logistics, in 1978 from Michigan State University. He is currently the Distinguished Professor of Logistics and the Harry J. and Vivienne R. Bruce Chair of Excellence in Business Policy in the Department of Marketing Logistics and Transportation at the University of Tennessee in Knoxville, Tennessee.

He has served as a consultant to over 50 corporations and government agencies, and is on the board of directors of several corporations. From 1969 to 1976 he worked for General Motors in various production and logistics management positions.

He is currently President of the Board of Directors of the Sheth Foundation and serves on the Board of Directors of both the Academy of Marketing Science Foundation and the American Marketing Association Foundation. He was formerly President and Vice President for Programs of the Academy of Marketing Science, and is a Distinguished Fellow of the Academy of Marketing Science – a distinction granted to fewer than twenty scholars worldwide.

Professor Mentzer has been a member of the Council of Logistics Management's Executive Committee since 1994, serving first as

Professional Development Chairperson. He then served as Research Strategies Chairperson in 1995 and 1996, General Conference Chairperson for the 1997 annual conference, Secretary and Treasurer in 1998, Second Vice President in 1999, and First Vice President in 2000.

Notable publications

As author of more than 130 papers and articles appearing in numerous journals and research reports, and co-author of five books, Professor Mentzer was recognized in 1996 as one of the five most prolific authors in the *Journal of the Academy of Marketing Science*, and in 1999 as the most prolific author in the *Journal of Business Logistics*.

He serves on the editorial review boards of various journals and previously served as editor of the systems section of the *Journal of Business Logistics*. He has most recently edited *Supply Chain Management* (Sage Publications Inc., 2001).

Patricia E. Moody

Patricia Moody has earned certification as a Certified Management Consultant (CMC) from the Institute of Management Consultants. *Fortune* magazine has named her one of the ten pioneering women in manufacturing.

Ms Moody holds a MBA from Simmons College Graduate School of Management. She spent seven years in industry purchasing, master scheduling, materials management and business planning, manufacturing systems design and implementation, at Simplex, Digital Equipment Corporation, and Data General. Her manufacturing management consulting work includes many top companies. She is a frequent public speaker.

As former editor of the Association of Manufacturing Excellence's (AME) magazine *Target* and a frequent contributor to *iSource*, *Sloan Management Review*, *Manufacturing Asia*, and other manufacturing and supply chain media, she has created breakthrough work on the future of manufacturing, teams, kaizen, new product development, supply management, and e-commerce and e-manufacturing. She is a member of the editorial advisory board of *Sloan Management Review*.

Notable publications

Besides her work as a manufacturing management consultant with over 30 years of industry, consulting and teaching experience, Ms Moody is also a many-time-published author. Her books include:

» *Strategic Manufacturing* (Dow Jones/Irwin, 1990);
» *Breakthrough Partnering* (John Wiley, 1993);
» *Leading Manufacturing Excellence* (John Wiley, 1997);
» (with Dave Nelson and Rick Mayo) *Powered by Honda: Developing Excellence in the Global Enterprise* (John Wiley, 1998);
» (with Robert W. Hall and Tony Laraia) *AME's Kaizen Blitz* (John Wiley, 1999);
» (with Dick Morley) *The Technology Machine* (Free Press, 1999);
» (with Dave Nelson) *The Purchasing Machine: How the Top Ten Companies Use Best Practices to Manage their Supply Chains* (Free Press/Simon & Schuster, 2000);
» (with Anand Sharma) *The Perfect Engine* (Free Press/Simon & Schuster, 2001).

NOTE

1 ''Industrial dynamics: a major breakthrough for decision makers,'' Harvard Business Review, July/August 1958, pp. 37-66.

Resources for Supply Chain Management

Countless words have been written about the subject of the supply chain. This chapter identifies the best supply chain resources:

» institutions, organizations, and associations;
» Websites; and
» journals, magazines, and books.

"The supply chain is very organic. You can see materials requirements planning, but we're still in the supply chain. It hasn't telescoped."

Patricia Moody, CMC

There is no lack of resources on supply chain management in print, on the Web, or in terms of associations and professional societies you can join. If anything, there is almost an over-abundance of resources on this topic. Information included in this chapter is culled from major associations and experts in the field. Note that it represents a mere skim of what is available for those interested in delving deeper.

ACADEMIC INSTITUTIONS NOTED FOR PROMOTING SUPPLY CHAIN STUDY

Although the supply chain is a global study, its main boosters are American. Four universities in the United States are considered the top places to learn about supply chain management. They are:

» Michigan State University
» Ohio State University
» Pennsylvania State University
» University of Tennessee (Knoxville).

KEY SOURCES

In print (magazines and journals)

Asked where they turn for cutting-edge and insightful supply chain thinking, the experts listed the following magazines and journals:

» *Global Sites & Logistics*
» *Global Logistics & Supply Chain Strategies*
» *Inbound Logistics*
» *International Journal of Supply Chain Management*
» *International Marketing*
» *International Journal of Physical Distribution*
» *Journal of Business Logistics* (Council of Logistics Management)

- » *Journal of Commerce* (now a logistics publication)
- » *Logistics Management*
- » *Reporter* (American National Standards Institute)
- » *Purchasing Magazine*
- » *Sloan Management Review*
- » *Supply Chain Brain*
- » *Supply Chain E-Business*
- » *Supply Strategy*
- » *Supply Chain Technology News*
- » *Supply Chain Management Review*
- » *Target* (Association of Manufacturing Excellence)
- » *Traffic Management Magazine*
- » *Traffic Technology International*
- » *Traffic World*
- » *Transportation & Distribution*
- » *Transport Topics* (American Trucking Association).

On the Web

The Web is a growing source of supply chain information. Here are some sites that the experts say are top-notch and packed with know-how:

- » www.supply-chain.org
- » www.supplystrategy.net (*Supply Strategy* Website)
- » www.totalsupplychain.com (Penton Publishing supply-chain resources)
- » www.supplychainbrain (Global Supply-Chain Media)
- » www.accenture.com (*Supply Chain Management Review* White Paper Collection).

See individual associations mentioned below. Most have Web pages with supply chain resources listed.

SEMINAL ARTICLES, BOOKS, AND VIDEOS

The following are culled from the Web archives of the Council of Logistics Management and *Supply Chain Management Review* (see Chapter 8 for additional publications):

Council of Logistics Management recommendations

» *Logistics Outsourcing: A Management Guide* (2000)
Covers important subject matters such as why outsource, what should be outsourced, developing an outsourcing strategy, selecting a provider, developing a contract, and implementation. $75 (members $40).

» *The Growth and Development of Logistics Personnel* (1999)
Addresses the growing importance of human resource issues in logistics and the need to understand the specifics of logistics jobs and how they fit into the ever-changing logistics field. $75 (members $40).

» *21st Century Logistics: Making Supply Chain Integration a Reality* (1999)
Written specifically for managers who face the challenge of developing corporate competitiveness in the coming decade through the power of supply chain management. $75 (members $40).

» *Keeping Score: Measuring the Business Value of Logistics in the Supply Chain* (1999)
Asks how well you "keep score" in logistics – that is, how well you measure the performance of your logistics operations. $75 (members $40).

» *Development and Implementation of Reverse Logistics Programs* (1998)
A "white paper" examining the components of the reverse logistics process and discusses how these processes can profitably "close the loop" on the supply chain. $75 (members $40).

» *Creating Logistics Value: Themes for the Future* (1995)
Research furthering our understanding of the conceptual relationships that pertain to the process of logistics value creation, and critically examines experiences of companies which have addressed issues relating to the measurement and quantification of logistics value. $75 (members $40).

» *Improving Quality and Productivity in the Logistics Process: Achieving Customer Satisfaction Breakthroughs* (1991)
Reveals key findings about how companies keep their customers satisfied. $75 (members $40).

» *Journal of Business Logistics* (two issues: spring/fall)

A journal having an editorial thrust toward applied, real-life articles with a blend of theoretical material. $75 (members $40).

» Annual conference proceedings

These contain a wide variety of articles on subjects relating to logistics management as presented at the conferences – 2000 (New Orleans, LA); 1999 (Toronto, Canada); 1998 (Anaheim, CA); 1997 (Chicago, IL); 1996 (Orlando, FL). $40 (members and nonmembers).

» *Logistics: Careers With A Challenge* (a half-hour VHS videotape)

Uses a pipeline analogy to describe a logistics system and is enhanced by comments from real-life logistics managers who explain what they do. It is directed at late high school and early college students. $35 (members and nonmembers).

» *Careers in Logistics* (1998)

A booklet providing information on the nature and importance of logistics careers, including salary information, where the jobs are, job profiles, and the education and training that is required. Single free copies are available to members and nonmembers.

Supply Chain Management Review recommendations

» *The Supply Chain Yearbook*, John A. Woods & Edward J. Maricn (eds), 2001.

» *Supply Chain Management*, John T. Mentzer, 2001.

» *The Supply Chain Network @ Internet Speed: Preparing Your Company for the E-Commerce Revolution*, Fred A. Kuglin & Barbara A. Rosenbaum, 2001.

» *Logistics Outsourcing: A Management Guide*, Clifford F. Lynch, 2000.

» *Trusted Partners: How Companies Build Mutual Trust and Win Together*, Jordan D. Lewis, 2000.

» *Alliance Competence: Maximizing the Value of Your Partnerships*, Robert E. Spekman & Lynn A. Isabella, 2000.

» *Designing and Managing the Supply Chain*, David Simchi-Levi, Philip Kaminsky, & Edith Simchi-Levi, 2000.

» *Blown to Bits: How the New Economics of Information Transforms Strategy*, Philip Evans & Thomas S. Wurster, 2000.

» The Education Society for Resource Management Website – www.apics.org, 2000.

NOTABLE SUPPLY CHAIN MANAGEMENT ASSOCIATIONS

The following are only a handful of associations from around the globe that cater to the supply chain and logistics industry. These are the recommendations of supply chain experts listed in Chapter 8, along with some examples from countries in Asia, Latin America, and Europe.

American Society of Transportation & Logistics

» A professional organization in which individuals hold membership.

Purpose/objective – To establish, promote, and maintain high standards of knowledge and professional training; to formulate a code of ethics for the profession; to advance the professional interest of members of the organization; to serve as a source of information and guidance for the fields of traffic, transportation, logistics, and physical distribution management; and to serve the industry as a whole by fostering professional accomplishments.
Membership – 1500
Contacts – tel: (203) 964-8645; fax: (203) 964-8688; e-mail: info@astl.org; www.astl.org
Address – 3 Landmark Square, Suite 401, Stamford, CT 06901, USA

American Trucking Associations Inc.

» A trade organization in which corporations hold membership.

Membership – 4500
Contacts – tel: (703) 838-1866; fax: (703) 684-5751; e-mail: wmcormick@trucking.org; www.trucking.org
Address – 2200 Mill Road, Alexandria, VA 22314, USA

APICS – The Educational Society for Resource Management

» A professional organization in which membership is extended on both an individual and corporate basis.

Purpose/objective – Founded in 1957 as the American Production and Inventory Control Society (hence APICS). The society has evolved to

meet the changing needs of business by providing broad-based individual and organizational education focused on integrating resources
for improved productivity. To reflect this mission, the society is now
known as APICS – The Educational Society for Resource Management.
It offers a full range of cost-effective, results-oriented education options
for the manufacturing and service sectors, including conferences
and seminars, books and publications, and professional certification
programs.

Membership – 13,300 corporate members plus 56,700 individual
members

Contacts – tel: (703) 354-8851; fax: (703) 354-8785; e-mail: j_raynes@
apics-hq.org; www.apics.org

Address – 5301 Shawnee Road, Alexandria, VA 22312, USA

ATA Information Technology & Logistics Council

» An organization in which membership is extended on both an
individual and a corporate basis.

Purpose/objective – The council is an organization of logistics professionals which exists to promote the industry and to create value for
members through education and advocacy.

Membership – 500 individual members

Contacts – tel: (703) 838-1766; fax: (703) 684-4328; e-mail: ckirk@truc-
king.org; www.trucking.org

Address – 2200 Mill Road, Alexandria, VA 22314, USA

Council of Logistics Management

» A professional organization in which individuals hold membership.

Purpose/objective – To provide: leadership in developing, defining,
understanding, and enhancing the logistics process on a worldwide
basis; a forum for the exchange of concepts and best practices among
logistics professionals; research that advances knowledge and leads to
enhanced customer value and supply chain performance; education
and career development programs that enhance career opportunities in logistics management. The council is an open organization
which offers individual membership to persons in all industries, types

of businesses, and job functions involved in the logistics process. In recognition of diversity, the council will give priority to actively involving individuals from currently under-represented populations in its activities. The council will operate on a not-for-profit, self-supporting basis, with emphasis on quality and in a cooperative manner with other organizations and institutions.

Membership – 15,000

Contacts – tel: (630) 574-0985; fax: (630) 574-0537; e-mail: mmcintyre@clm1.org; www.clm1.org

Address – 2805 Butterfield Road, Suite 200, Oak Brook, IL 60523, USA

Deutsche Gesellschaft für Logistik e.v.

» An organization in which membership is extended on both an individual and a corporate basis.

Purpose/objective – To promote scientific and practical research and development in the field of logistics, with particular consideration of industry, commerce and services, and educational programming.

Membership – 800 individual members and 200 corporate members

Contacts – tel: (49) 231 9700 120; fax: (49) 231 9700 464; e-mail: dgflev@t-online.de; www.dgfl.de

Address – Dortmund 44227, Germany

Grocery Manufacturers of America Inc.

» A trade association in which corporations hold membership.

Contacts – tel: (202) 337-9400; Fax: (202) 337-4508; e-mail: cmm@gmabrands.com; www.gmabrands.org

Address – 1010 Wisconsin Avenue NW, Washington, DC 20007, USA

Institut International de Management pour la Logistique

» A professional organization in which corporations hold membership.

Purpose/objective – To promote the development and use of logistical organization methods through education and research; to participate in the development of procedures concerning international trade; to train high-level managers in the field of logistics; to introduce young people to the methodical, instrumental, and practical foundations of the field of logistics.

Membership – 60

Contacts – tel: (21) 693-2465; fax: (21) 693-5060; e-mail: francis-luc. perret@epfl.ch; www.epfl.ch

Address – CH-1015 Lausanne, Switzerland

International Air Cargo Association

» An organization in which companies, allied trade associations, and individuals hold membership.

Purpose/objective – To champion the causes of the air logistics industry, promote unity and mutual cooperation among its members, and advance the industry's role as a major power in world trade. The association serves as the primary voice and force for positive change and fair practices, and provides key leadership for all interests in expanding global commerce through air distribution.

Contacts – tel: (305) 443-9696; e-mail: secgen@tiaca.org; www.tiaca.org

Address – 3111 SW 27th Avenue, PO Box 330669, Coconut Grove, Miami, FL 33233-0669, USA

Japan Institute of Logistics Systems

» An organization in which membership is extended on both an individual and a corporate basis.

Purpose/objective – To contribute to the development of the national economy and to develop activities relating to the modernization of logistics; to promote logistics systems in the commercial field; to conduct seminars, workshops, and conferences, and to sponsor overseas tours that are of interest to logistics management personnel.

Membership – 860 corporate members and 60 individual members.

Contacts – tel: (81) 3 3432-3291; fax: (81) 3 3432-8681; e-mail: kakuta@logistics.or.jp; www.logistics.or.jp/jils

Address – Sumitomo Higashi-shinbashi Building 3, Goukan, 1-10-14 Hamamatsu-cho, Minato-ku, Tokyo 105-0013, Japan

Logistics Association of Australia

» A professional organization in which individuals hold membership.

Purpose/objective – The LAA is an association representing the interests of those involved in logistics. This includes warehousing distribution, purchasing, marketing, sales, customer service, and materials managers. The aim of increasing the professionalism of members is achieved by acting as the representative body for managers engaged in logistics functions; providing opportunities for interaction and sharing of experiences with other professionals; conducting monthly meetings to discuss topics and issues of interest; and providing opportunities for learning through participation in seminars, site visits, and tertiary courses.

Membership – 2000

Contacts – tel: (2) 9635-3422; fax: (2) 9635-3466; e-mail: logadmin@ logassoc.asn.au; www.logadmin.asn.au

Address – PO Box 249, Parramatta, NSW 2124, Australia

National Association of Purchasing Management Inc.

» An educational and research organization in which individuals hold membership.

Purpose/objective – The association is committed to providing national and international leadership on purchasing and materials management. Through its 181 affiliated associations, the association provides opportunities for purchasing and supply management practitioners to expand their professional skills and knowledge, and works to foster a better understanding of purchasing and supply management concepts.

Membership – 44,000

Contacts – tel: (480) 752-6276; fax: (480) 752-7890; e-mail: pnovak@ napm.org; www.napm.org

Address – PO Box 22160, Tempe, AZ 85285-2160, USA

National Association of Wholesaler-Distributors

» A trade association in which corporations hold membership.

Purpose/objective – The association is composed of Direct Member companies and a federation of national, regional, state, and local associations and their members firms which, collectively, total more than 45,000 companies. NAW's core mission is to advocate its members' interests on national policy issues which affect the entire wholesale distribution industry. In addition to its government relations program, NAW's scope encompasses the activities of the Wholesaler-Distributor Political Action Committee (WDPAC), the Distribution Research and Education Foundation (DREF), and the NAW Service Corporation (NAWSC).

Membership – 1000

Contacts – tel: (202) 872-0885; fax: (202) 785-0586; e-mail: naw@nawd. org; www.naw.org

Address – 1725 K Street NW, Washington, DC 20006, USA

National Industrial Transportation League

» Carriers and other service providers are eligible for associate status.

Purpose/objective – The NITL is the oldest and largest broad-based shippers' organization in the US. Founded in 1907, it is a voluntary organization of shippers, shippers' associations, boards of trade, chambers of commerce, and other entities concerned with the purchasing of freight transportation services. It is the only nationwide organization representing shippers of all sizes and commodities using all modes of transportation to move their goods via intrastate, interstate, and international commerce.

Membership – 1700 members

Contacts – tel: (703) 524-5011; fax: (703) 524-5017; e-mail: emmett@ nitl.org; www.nitl.org

Address – 1700 N. Moore Street, Suite 1900, Arlington, VA 22209-1904, USA

National Customs Brokers & Forwarders Association of America

» A trade association in which corporations hold membership.

Purpose/objective – To represent the licensed customs brokers, international freight forwarders, and international air cargo agents located throughout the US.

Membership – 600+
Contacts – tel: (202) 466-0222; fax: (202) 466-0226; e-mail: breilly@ncbfaa.org; www.ncbfaa.org
Address – 1200 18th Street NW, Suite 901, Washington, DC 20009, USA

Supply Chain Council Inc.

» A trade association in which corporations hold membership.

Purpose/objective – The council was incorporated in 1977 as a global, not-for-profit trade association with membership open to all companies interested in improving supply chain efficiencies through the use of the Supply Chain Operations Reference model.
Membership – 550
Contacts – tel: (412) 781-4101; fax: (412) 781-2871; e-mail: bill@hakanson.com; www.supply-chain.org
Address – 303 Freeport Road, Pittsburgh, PA 15215, USA

Transportation Research Board

» An organization in which membership is extended on both an individual and corporate basis.

Purpose/objective – To advance knowledge concerning the nature and performance of transportation systems by stimulating research and disseminating the information derived from research.
Membership – 2200 individuals and 200 corporations
Contacts – tel: (202) 334-2936; fax: (202) 334-2920; e-mail: bskinner@x2nas.edu; www.nas.edu/trb
Address – 2101 Constitution Avenue NW, Washington, DC 20418, USA

Transportation Research Forum

» A professional organization in which individuals hold membership.

Purpose/objective – To provide an impartial meeting ground for carriers, shippers, government, officials, consultants, university researchers, suppliers, and others seeking an exchange of information and ideas related to both passengers and freight transportation.

Membership – 400
Contacts – tel: (202) 879-4701; fax: (202) 879-4719; e-mail: rob@eno-trans.com
Address – 1 Farragut Square South, Suite 500, Washington, DC 20006-4003, USA

Uruguayan Logistics Association (URULOG)

» A professional organization in which individuals hold membership.

Purpose/objective – To promote logistics in Uruguay. URULOG organizes several activities concerning material handling, ports, supply chains, warehousing, transport etc.
Membership – 100
Contacts – tel: (82) 307-6873; (82) 400-2100; e-mail: urulog@montevideo.com.uy
Address – Av. Rivera 2203/601, 11600 Montevideo, Uruguay

Warehousing Education and Research Council

» A professional organization in which individuals hold membership.

Purpose/objective – To provide education and to conduct research concerning the warehousing process; and to refine the art and science of managing warehouses. WERC aims to foster professionalism in warehouse management. It operates without profit and in cooperation with other organizations and institutions.
Membership – 4000
Contacts – tel: (630) 990-0001; fax: (630) 990-0256; e-mail: sbova@werc.org; www.werc.org
Address – 1100 Jorie Boulevard, Suite 170, Oak Brook, IL 60523–2243, USA

Ten Steps to Making the Supply Chain Work

Supply chain theory is one thing; putting it into practice is another. This chapter provides some key insights into creating/sustaining a supply chain in today's business environment, including sections on:

» maintaining just-in-time;
» thinking collaboration, thinking demand pipeline;
» maintaining quality;
» information management;
» managing change;
» new roles;
» selecting the right technology;
» organizing now for the supply network future;
» moving to a Web environment; and
» building a Web presence.

"The toughest part of this whole supply chain trend involves something as simple as candor and humility . . . To be able to go to a supplier you've beaten up over the years and say we know you're farther ahead on the technology front than we are and would like to do everything possible to set up an alliance with you. This takes the sort of humility and candor, what's required of a monk."

Jim Morgan[1]

Those who sign on to the concept of supply chain revolution find out quickly that revolution means change. Especially important is a new managerial approach that is less hierarchical, more communicative, and more empowering of employees. So the tools of the supply chain revolution become communication, employee empowerment, quality, information management, and the ability to select the right technology and prepare your company to handle them. Here are ten steps to making today's supply chain work, which means gearing up to operate a supply network.

Most of the material in this chapter is adapted from the author's *Supply Chain Survival Kit* (A–Z International, Amherst, MA. © 1999)

1. MAINTAIN JUST-IN-TIME

To maintain just-in-time shipping and manufacturing schedules, it's becoming imperative to provide real-time information on where shipments are located at any given time.

EDI, or an EDI/Internet combination, are among key tools manufacturer/shippers and transport professionals use to link operations and keep tabs on shipments. More and more, though, satellites are providing the same information, which is then posted on carrier and logistics company Websites for ongoing, real-time tracking of shipments. Cellular technology, used to transmit both voice and data, is used in areas where fixed lines are not available.

Satellite technology is coming into its own, moving out of the realm of NASA and the defense department and into the cabs of trucks and dispatch offices throughout the United States. Companies from American Mobile Satellite, to Qualcomm, Orbcomm, and

Rockwell, are exploring a vast number of uses for their equipment – ranging from tracking, tracing, security, emergency communication, and preventive maintenance to the transmission of freight bills, fleet management, and the automatic tracking of state highway taxes – anything that will work to give their customers a competitive edge.

2. THINK COLLABORATION; THINK DEMAND PIPELINE

Analysts predict that c-commerce will become the dominant norm in less than five years. They believe you should start preparing your companies and institutions now by extending, opening, and securing your applications architecture to be able to integrate with a wider universe of potential business partners. That means working with vendors focused on your industry, and who can ensure that there is a match between your primary needs and their core expertise. And they believe that software and other technology vendors will develop products to support this vision that are related to specific market niches. The game plan is to align with vendors that can demonstrate a specific focus in your industry.

The move to B2B and a supply network means learning about collaboration and taking a team approach. Long-held views about fighting the competition may have to be altered. Ways of sharing information with competitors, while maintaining a competitive stance, will have to be developed electronically. Making these sorts of changes will mean offering incentives to employees.

Other experts are taking collaboration beyond the supply chain and creating what they call a ''demand pipeline.'' In the world of the demand pipeline, manufacturers and their suppliers are looking for:

''. . . fundamentally different operating processes to replace traditional point-to-point, multi-stop, hierarchical, inventory-intensive materials-handling processes. They are beginning to collaborate to develop synchronized response systems that emulate networks of pipelines rather than point-to-point chains. Along these virtual pipelines, they look to minimize the number of inventory pools needed to assure supply. Importantly, they are gearing the level of inventory in each pool as closely as possible to the actual outflow of material from that pool. The result is best thought of as a network of demand pipelines, rather than as links in a chain."

Fred Hewitt[2]

3. MAINTAIN QUALITY

Supply chain executives know that maintaining high quality is key to keeping to a just-in-time manufacturing and shipping schedule. The more defects there are in raw materials, components, and finished goods, the more the supply chain bogs down.

As an auto-industry executive explains, you cannot get cost and timing if the quality component is not there. Consider this scenario: A piece of raw material has to move through a variety of manufacturing processes before it becomes part of a finished product in a showroom. That raw metal has to move through the production process totally defect-free to avoid slow-downs on the production line.

If all of a sudden it becomes defective, and you have to move another piece, then you're not going to meet response time. That product flowing through the supply chain becomes absolutely critical to making that response time work. Awareness of how quality affects costs has meant a switch from using quality as a marketing tool to using quality as a cost-containment tool.

Emphasis on quality processes becomes more crucial in a supply network where suppliers are more and more responsible for design, as well as manufacturing. The more an organization focuses on maintaining high quality levels and adopts quality management systems, the smoother the supply chain will run. Quality becomes an enabler of this fast response time and short cycle times.

4. MANAGE INFORMATION

With more and more outsourcing of manufacturing and more component parts being sought, companies are finding that sophisticated information management is becoming a key ingredient for success. Problems arise when companies turn to technology as a panacea and ignore the fact that technology is only a tool. Here are some real-life examples.

» A multinational corporation attempts to link global suppliers with EDI and finds its transmissions riddled with errors and not sent on a timely basis.

» A computer giant is experiencing e-mail gridlock because it hasn't strategically assessed how to employ technology as part of a company-wide communication system.

Increasing use of advanced technologies requires companies to think in terms of information management. To get the greatest bang from their technology investments, companies need to be able to gather, sort, store, cull and disseminate data, information, and knowledge. They need to be able to analyze and break out information into useful units to be applied strategically. And they have to be able to set up information/communication chains to match work flow, whether regional or global.

5. MANAGE CHANGE

All the advanced technology in the world will not create a perfectly flowing supply chain. At the heart of supply chains, value nets, or webs, and a supply network, are people. And that means there's a psychology to the supply chain that must be addressed for the best laid plans to function. The issue is helping employees – top management on down – to cope with the changes that the collaborative atmosphere of the Web is bringing to many organizations.

Throwing technology at what are fundamentally human issues won't solve your cost-containment problems, as failure rates of enterprise resource planning (ERP) software have indicated. To successfully utilize advanced technology, or practice e-commerce, the experts contend that top management must embrace technology change and the supply network mentality. Then they must "forge a new relationship with their own employees, especially the purchasing manager and their suppliers, if they are to reap competitive rewards."[3]

Are managers globally prepared to make this shift? Certainly many companies – from the Big Three automakers to Texas Instruments and Bell Helicopter and Nortel – are recognizing that promoting improved communication is key to supply chain flow. And manufacturers of supply chain related software are recognizing their products may directly affect how a company is managed. That's why SAP, for example, is working with Ernst & Young management consultants as part of their implementation scheme.

STEPS REQUIRED TO MANAGE CHANGE IN A SUPPLY NETWORK ENVIRONMENT

» Break down hierarchical structures to allow for information sharing and true collaboration among employees and then throughout a supply network.

» Create new management positions to ensure proper use of technology throughout your organization.

» Improve communication skills so that management clearly expresses priorities.

» Build customer relationships rather than only providing customer service.

» Establish new rules of communication so that the vast amount of information that technology makes available can be used for maximum purpose, and not overwhelm an organization.[4]

6. RECOGNIZE NEW ROLES

The supply chain revolution is creating new roles for many people in an organization, not to mention new industries. Advanced technologies are changing the way people do their work, as well as creating new jobs. When General Motors hired its first information technology chief a few years ago, he promptly advertised for 300 chief information officers to fill slots at the company. It is not uncommon to hear of companies today appointing chief knowledge officers.

With the advent of business-to-business (B2B) electronic commerce, the purchasing role is changing drastically. Some purchasing managers now head up parts of their organization's logistics operations to better track costs.

Other new roles are emerging all the time. For example, Xerox recently decided to create the position of customer supply assurance manager (CSAM).

''The CSAM's role reflects the belief that effectiveness and efficiency stem as much from integrated decision making as from integrated physical materials handling. Matching supply to demand in real time now is the responsibility of a professional, not a committee.''

Fred Hewitt[5]

7. SELECT THE RIGHT TECHNOLOGY

With an estimated 60–80% failure rate among IT solutions, it's imperative to select the technology that not only works, but best matches your supply chain needs. One factor to consider is adopting a technology mindset. Technology consultants are learning that the degree to which managers are willing to change directly affects what technology solutions they are willing to choose.

Tying technology choices to organizational goals is also crucial to making IT choices. New technology releases are taking place daily, or so it seems. The technology experts say not to change technology without a cost justification that directly ties into your organizational goals. And while you're at it, make sure your staff are comfortable with the technology you pick.

Microsoft, for example, has been pushing new releases of Windows® just about every other year or even annually. Some organizations find employees have not adjusted to Windows 95 when they're being asked to work in Windows 2000. This leads to feelings of incompetence and discomfort within an organization. Rolling out the latest and greatest technology may destabilize your organization. So assessing employee comfort levels will be one indication of when to make change.[6]

8. ORGANIZE NOW FOR THE SUPPLY NETWORK FUTURE

You will not succeed in developing a supply network to compete in a B2B, Web-based environment if you haven't networked their organization and, as part of that effort, integrated business functions in an electronic fashion. Even if you choose to outsource back-office functions, you still need your operation to run flexibly and efficiently and to create databases to store information. Before you start plunking down cash for servers and database applications and solutions, consider integrating the technologies you already have using the niche ware and middleware.

The following are two key steps to organizing for the supply network future.

» Adopt ERP principles. Analysts believe one of the best strategies for this evolving into a networked, B2B organization to is adopt the principles of ERP without necessarily buying into a full ERP software solution. Or, alternatively, you can purchase those portions of ERP solutions that help you integrate whatever functions you don't choose to outsource. Why bother with ERP? Let's face it, the Internet has not developed to that all-encompassing tool that will eliminate the need for translators, middleware and the like. ERP can be the quickest and easiest way for small and mid-size companies to find a way to integrate a host of applications.

» Know alternative ways to manage integration: For many companies, the world has become an electronic hodge-podge of incompatible systems. What you need to be considering is integration – or the act of taking data from one software application (output), and without human intervention, using it as input into a separate application. Besides ERP tools, there are also supply chain planning and execution tools available on the market. These promote collaboration beyond your company or institution. They will allow for your systems to communicate, which is the basis of the networked, B2B world that you are working to build.[7]

9. MOVE TO A WEB ENVIRONMENT

Once you have your technology in place to operate a facsimile supply network, it's time to start talking to your suppliers and bringing them into your c-commerce vision. Institutions might start talking to other organizations that offer collaborative advantage. You need to study how to integrate your activities – and what activities you want to integrate – using the Internet as a communication tool.

Even though you may be conducting negotiations with suppliers and collaboration partners for months to come, it's not too soon to get members of your organization prepared to operate in a c-commerce fashion. This will involve a great deal of the management work, particularly developing an open work culture where information is shared, and striving for collaboration not competition.[8]

Your next step to moving into a Web environment is picking the Web activities that build your organization. That may mean buying your logistics services through an ASP, procuring goods through an online auction, exchange or marketplace. What matters is that you get out there in cyberspace and explore new options for cutting costs throughout your supply chain and emerging supply network.

10. BUILD A WEB PRESENCE

Part of working in a collaborative supply network environment means building a Web presence, which might include a Website, product catalogs, and whatever tools you need for online action. Don't get down on yourself if you haven't yet established a Web presence. It's better to move into the Web-based, supply network world slowly and determinedly than to toss up a quickie home page with no purpose behind it.

Remember, only a tiny percentage of major companies use their sites to develop and maintain a relationship with their customers. And only a small percentage use the most advanced Internet technologies to offer real-time business processing for functions like financial management and human resources. The Web is a phenomenal outreach tool that can help contain costs and build you profit, but only if smart business sense prevails. Think of your Web presence as a tool to improve supply chain management, not a cure-all, and ways of using this new tool will quickly become apparent.

KEY LEARNING POINTS

» Maintaining just-in-time schedules means employing the most effective technology that you can afford and then setting up information flow systems to ensure timely and accurate transmissions.

» Start thinking collaboration among all supply chain members.

» Poor quality management can bring a supply chain to a halt. If you don't have a quality management system in place, it's time to move in that direction – fast.

» You had better be able to manage change because the evolution from a supply chain to a Web-based supply network is here and new developments are taking place daily.

» Be prepared to create new roles in your organization to handle the needs of a Web-enabled world, with a particular emphasis on information management and procurement.

» Selecting the right technology to match your business goals is key to success.

» Organizing your operation and training employees to function in a networked, Web environment is one of the most important steps you can take to maintain a competitive supply chain.

» Start assessing how you can move to a Web environment, whether that means exploring e-procurement or downloading logistics management software from an ASP.

» Building a Web presence, even a billboard Website, is something to start doing today.

NOTES

1 Editorial Director Emeritus, *Purchasing Magazine*; quoted in the author's *Supply Chain Survival Kit.*

2 "After supply chains, think demand pipelines" by Fred Hewitt, *Supply Chain Management Review*, online edition, June 11, 2001.

3 Jim Morgan, as note 1.

4 Reproduced from the author's *Tech Trending* in the ExpressExec series. The source is David Washburn, Principal Consultant at Amherst Information Architects, Amherst, MA.

5 Fred Hewitt, *ibid.*

6 David Washburn, as note 4.

7 Reproduced from the author's *Tech Trending* in the ExpressExec series. The sources are Henry Bruce, Vice President of Marketing, Optum Software, White Plains, NY; and Deborah Wilson, Deborah Wilson Consulting.

8 Reproduced from the author's *Tech Trending* in the ExpressExec series. The source is Kevin Fitzgerald, Editor-in-Chief, *Supply Strategy* magazine.

Frequently Asked Questions (FAQs)

Q1: What is the supply chain?

A: Refer to Chapters 1 and 2.

Q2: How does logistics fit into the supply chain?

A: Refer to the section on logistics in Chapter 2.

Q3: When did the term "supply chain" come into being?

A: Refer to the opening section of Chapter 3.

Q4: How has technology affected supply chain development?

A: Refer to Chapter 3 on the emergence of a supply network and Chapter 4 on the e-dimension.

Q5: What does it take to operate a global supply chain?

A: Refer to Chapter 5.

Q6: How is the world of procurement and sourcing changing?

A: Refer to Chapter 4.

Q7: What technology will I need to move to a supply network?

A: Refer to Chapter 6 on moving from a supply chain to a supply network.

Q8: Who are the key players in the supply chain movement and where can I find resources to guide me?

A: Refer to Chapters 8 and 9.

Q9: What are supply chain tools and enablers I can use to run a more efficient supply chain?

A: Refer to the best-practice section in Chapter 4, and Chapter 10.

Q10: What are some best practices available from successful supply chain implementations?

A: Refer to the best-practice section in Chapter 4.

Index